STORY SQUAD

Education Boutique
A BESPOKE TUTORING SOLUTION

These stories are works of fiction. Names, characters, places and incidents either are the product of the authors imaginations or are used fictitiously. Any resemblance to actual persons, living or dead, events or locales is entirely coincidental.

Copyright © 2020 by Education Boutique

All rights reserved.

No part of this book may be reproduced or used in any manner without written permission of the copyright owner.

Proof Reader: Brooke McClure

Cover Design: Lucy Spencer

ISBN 9798652790868

www.educationboutique.co.uk

TABLE OF CONTENTS

Preface	1
The Encounter, *by Max Kan*	2
Courageous David, *by Brij Shah*	5
Race to Remember, *by Aarya Kolpyakwar*	7
Honesty is the Best Policy! *by Rahul Maddipatla*	9
The Time Crystal: Herbajerbs are from Venus, *by Jessica Chambers*	11
A Treasure Island, *by Arnay Gupta*	14
The Golden Treasure, *by Declan McQuillan Woodhouse*	17
Journeying Through Video Games, *by Roshni Syed Rafiq*	19
The World Between the Two Trees, *by Imani Egau*	21
Around the World in 80 Rides, *by Mia Bhute*	23
The S Pendant, *by Diya Nair*	25
Bobbie and The Ruby Staff of the Pyramid, *by Prahen Mahendran*	26
Speedoaster vs Tricker, *by Sumant Rathi*	30
The House, *by Andrew Popescu*	33
The Tommies Dark Side, *by Aaryan Goyal*	35
Trapped, *by Riya Goyal*	36
Deep Dark Death, *by Bisam Kaur*	37
The Dangerous Journey, *by Ane Jekabson*	39
The Invisible Guest, *by Sreehari Anoop*	40
The Toy Box, *by Hasini Vangapalli*	41
The Tunnel, *by Shenul De Silva*	43
Trapped, *by Riya Shah*	44
Checkmate, *by Shnaya Singh*	45
Hermione and Hydra, *by Emma Giol Butnaru*	47
The Race, *by Vihaan Mohan*	49
The Boy Who Said Yes, *by George Fowler*	52
The Mansion, *by Anneliese Gambrill*	53
The Cursed Secret, *by Eloisa Beasant*	55
A Lucky Escape, *by Sia Rao*	57
Legend of Fangs, *by Sharon Cheruvathur*	58
Race You to the Alps, *by Krish Pathak*	59
Alex's Adventure, *by Mohammed Falahul Islam*	62
Demon's Playhouse, *by Max Yeoman*	64
Terror in the Mud, *by Dylan Yeoman*	66
Stranded on an Island, *by Ankit Kathare*	69
The Great Cure, *by Rohan Sai Kurumaddala*	70
The Light of day, *by Khyati Rahul Oza*	75
Lost, *by Anoushka Richard*	77
The Runaway Rat, *by Chahat Gupta*	79
The Magical Tree, *by Haziq Rizwan*	81
The Story of the Woods, *by Bella Young*	84

Preface

In the Spring of 2020, Covid-19 caused much uncertainty around the UK. Life as we knew it seemed to change overnight and no one was left unaffected; children could not attend school, parents were trying to figure out new working arrangements, leisure activities were not an option and we couldn't visit family and friends. Our daily routines were gone in the blink of an eye and we were left to adjust to a temporary, new normal.

Education Boutique was no different and had to find ways to adapt to this new way of life, so we made the move to online learning and created a Virtual School, starting with Creative Writing classes.

We were so impressed with our budding authors that we thought we would give students the opportunity to become published writers!

Story Squad is a compilation of stories written by children age 6-12. Children were able to submit a piece of writing that they were proud of, on any topic.

We are proud of the hard work these children have put into their stories and the dedication they have shown to the project. Feedback from parents, confirmed that this opportunity has motivated and inspired their children's learning and we are honoured that we could assist these 40 students in this small way during such uncertain times.

All proceeds from the sale of this book will be donated to the NHS, who we are ever grateful to during these unprecedented times.

We hope you enjoy reading *Story Squad*!

The Education Boutique Team

The Encounter

By Max Kan, Year 5

Viridian trees stood tall and proud as a boy had his eyes glued to the tranquil scene. Securely slung over his shoulders hung a robust navy backpack decorated with vibrant coral orange zips. The scenery's tranquillity delivered the sweet taste of joy. Trees grew in a perfect position to create a picturesque postcard. A gentle breeze caressed him causing a quiet whistle to blow into ears. As fish glided through the chartreuse lake, ripples disturbed its still surface. Light, fluffy clouds floated through the teal sky whilst the saffron sun beamed down. As he brought his gaze upwards, a gaping pathway cutting through the colossal forest appeared within his vision.

All of a sudden, he thought he saw a movement. What was it? Wondering what it was, the boy, Alex focused on the exact same spot, his cerulean eyes glued to the point. Emerald green leaves danced on gusts of air also blowing his beige hair. Meticulously, he picked up a stone and hurled it towards the tree's viridian cloaks. Over there! Brittle twigs snapped as branches swayed and leaves rustled. Hesitating, he toyed with the idea of investigating closer but decided against it. After lobbing a smaller pebble, he looked closer. This time seeing two mammoth beady eyes staring back at him.

Curiosity urged him to probe further but waiting at home was home-made curry; the aroma wafted through the air to his nostrils. Ravenous, he felt so hungry he could eat a horse. As he entered the house, it struck him: what had eyes that big? His curious personality forced him to explore and all he could think about before sleep was what it might be.

Slowly, he opened his eyes with the memories of the previous day's events throbbing in his head. Deciding he would investigate today, he leapt out of his blissful bed. Dressed, he sprinted downstairs, grabbed a bowl, took a spoon, poured himself some crunchy cereal and devoured it. Something told him to bring a weapon, but he decided bringing an item from home would be too conspicuous. Approaching the wooden azure front door, he thought he might find a sharp stick in the forest.

As he neared the same area of the park where he watched with intrigue yesterday, he found a moderately sized stick that was as sharp as a spear. Now he would head towards the chartreuse forest. Branches spread and twisted forming a prehistoric beast. Rustling of leaves reminded him of a real rainforest.

What was that? Definitely, he wasn't seeing things. Venturing on, he gripped his stick tighter. Soon he found what seemed to be a malfunctioning spaceship. Immediately an animal leapt out like a cheetah pouncing on its prey. Or was it something else? Yes! An alien seeming to beckon him to come towards the ship.

Cautiously, he skulked into the spacecraft and noticed perplexing buttons. Thinking Alex would understand, the alien spoke an unknown language. Realising he didn't, the alien busily started to build something. His arms as fast as lightning. Screws and spare bits flew everywhere. They landed on the ground making a loud thumping noise. Ingeniously, the alien had instantly built a translation machine.

They could communicate. Obviously, this alien was far more advanced than humans. But why was he here?

"Hello," he uttered, "I need heat to power my rocket ship."

"Ok," replied Alex, "I shall help." But how could he help? Fire will produce smoke and will make it obvious we are here. Alex was not one to give up but it seemed impossible. With determination, he decided he must help this alien. 'How?' ruminated in his head.

Something struck him; when he rubbed his hands together, which he often did when thinking, they felt warm. Could friction be creating the heat? Searching for an answer, his eyes fell upon the extraordinary alien. "Does friction cause heat?" He enquired.

"Yes," the alien answered excitedly, "I shall try to invent a machine to create and harness the power." Friction can generate heat without smoke - the perfect solution.

Whilst the alien set to work, Alex ambled around the ship curious about the controls onboard. Complicated wires led to a sophisticated helmet. Everything was written in unidentified symbols. Spinning like a dog chasing its tail but extremely rapid, he saw a control button moving.

Fingers creeping forward to press it, he was suddenly transported into a spiral of vibrant colourful lights. Almost at once, he landed back on Earth but he could see dinosaurs! Possibilities about what had happened floated to him but his mind settled on one. Amazingly, this alien could travel in time! In his sight, a colossal dinosaur charging after another smaller Stegosaurus. He felt dwarfed by the dangerous dinosaurs devouring each other. Without warning, the larger dinosaur's eyes turned to him. Pounding, his heart started to race around. But, with sudden relief, he was back in the safety of the spaceship. "Don't touch anything" the alien ordered. "Look," he pointed at a gigantic machine, but it wouldn't create friction without a coarse surface.

Alex jousted with this problem all night before falling asleep on the sofa.

The dawn of a new day was grey and overcast. Today, he would find something rough to produce heat for his alien. Walking towards his dad's workshop, he felt the wind stroke him and trees wave at him. Noisily, the door squealed as it crept open. Scattered, everywhere was sandpaper because his dad was a carpenter. There were two huge piles, and he would take them all to the alien. The alien needed it more, of course.

"Thank you" the alien responded with gratitude and diligently placed both piles onto the mechanical structure that it had constructed yesterday. Suddenly, the machine started to move, generating heat. Accelerating, until it was as fast as sound, a buzzing noise erupted from the machine. Hot sand flew through the air landing on his skin causing a pleasant tingling, burning sensation. With the sweet taste of success tickling his taste buds, the spaceship gradually roared and soared. Soon, there was no evidence of any alien landing, except a few indentations in the squelching soil and the communication machine that they had used to talk. Sadness and emptiness filled Alex when he wrapped his hands around the extraordinary translator and journeyed home.

That night, laying in his bed, a sound echoed through the room from the translator, "Alex!" it cried out...

Courageous David

By Brij Shah, 9 years old

Once upon a time, there lived a young boy called David. He lived with his Auntie whose name was Rose. They lived in a city called Derbyshire which is located in England. They lived in a small cottage where everything was normal.

David's parents left the young boy behind with Rose because he behaved very badly to everyone. He was a notorious boy who used to answer back to his parents and was excluded from many schools. Also, he used to bully many children during his previous schools. David's parents lived in Wales. They did not miss David that much.

His auntie Rose used to say, *"Life is not meant to be easy, my child; but take courage — it can be delightful."*

On a dark, dismal and dreadful night, a terrorist broke in. He came to take revenge on David because the terrorist's son got harassed a lot when they were in the same school. The cruel man hurt David.

"Help, help! Somebody come and save me!" David kept on shouting loudly.

Rose was in a deep sleep but she was woken up by the noise and asked, "What's that noise?" She thought it was David shouting about him losing in his game.

The man finally ran away after a few minutes. The house was as suspiciously silent as death and Rose looked down... David was unconscious! His eyes were shut tightly and blood was spread all over the floor. Rose couldn't believe her eyes! She never gave up. She called the police and ambulance.

The man got arrested. Luckily, David was alright after a few days. He was very grateful to his aunt for helping him recover. He made a goal in his life to save people's lives like his aunt Rose did.

A few days after the incident, Rose unfortunately passed away due to a heart attack. Rose meant so much to David. She was an inspirational lady to him.

A few hours later, he was found crying alone by a neighbour from out of the window. He went to many meetings and interviews. News about David was spread all over the country.

Days later, David got his parents back! His parents were sorry for leaving him behind because they knew that David would be suffering without them. This changed his life and the way he saw things. He was so happy to have a big house, nice family and all that he wished for. But there was only one thing he wanted now: freedom for his country. From that day, he improved his behaviour and started respecting his parents and everyone else too.

Strangely, many people went missing from his neighbourhood and violence was widely spread in his town. This was very strange and shocking for David.

Also, World War 2 had started. When David was old enough to survive by himself, he joined the army. From his young age, David started developing his strength and courage for joining the army. In World War 2, he fought bravely against his enemies.

After the victory of Britain (1945), David received a National Reward for defending our country and saving the lives of people. He inspired many people to be brave and courageous like him. Like others, his family were very proud of him. David learned a life lesson to always be good. He dedicated this reward to his late Auntie Rose and his parents for encouraging him to be brave, strong and to succeed in his life. He was a kind person who saved the lives of many people in human history. He was a hero for what he did and he succeeded in his life.

Bravery Triumphs!

Race to Remember

By Aarya Kolpyakwar, Year 5

Boom Boom! Hearts could be heard like a treacherous thunderstorm, not because of the people's anxiousness, but because of their athletic build and their hearts always roared louder than a lion.

Dumbfounded, he questioned why he had ever agreed to take part in this challenge; he was the youngest there! Life drained from his face, his jaw hit the floor… "This can't be right!" He surprisingly blurted out. SILENCE! No one moved, everyone glared at him, stared right into his azure eyes. He turned tomato red. To avoid any more embarrassment, he decided to go in the crowd nearby and not do anything that was not thought out.

Reluctantly, he picked up his 100-ton bag and apprehensively checked it. "My mother had warned me to make my decisions carefully and I did it without thinking, I cannot believe she was right," he grumbled to himself. "I would have been at home playing my precious video game, if only…if only…"

After the hurricane of people calmed, the athletes carefully examined the maps making sure they were going the right way, this was not a pleasant time for Oliver as he was missing everything, even his annoying little sister. Most of the people had gone to a hotel to spend the night and he could not possibly book one as no one would let him. So, he slept in a rotting dumpster as he had no other choice.

This race went across many hills and mountains all the way to Italy. But you could not take a flight to Cinque, Terre, Italy. And of course, the first one there would be the winner and they would get their hands on the 50,000 pounds. But Oliver's goal wasn't that, it was to win money for his mum's cancer treatment.

3.. 2.. 1.. GO!

Groaning, he reluctantly pulled himself up, Oliver had cramps all over and he smelt as bad as a rotten egg from sleeping in the dilapidated dumpster. "Has my alarm clock buzzed?" He said in a hoarse voice. "Come on, come on get ready two minutes," voice cut through the silence, it was the commentator. "This isn't going to be fun, huh! I wish that man would stop babbling that nonsense, I better get up NOW!" Oliver screamed furiously. Yanking his hair out he stood up and pulled his coat on.

Stumbling, to the starting line the crowd bombarded in front of him shoving him vigorously, to the coarse wall.

"3!" shouted the starter.

"Wait," but no one could hear his mournful cries.

"2, 1, GO!"

"Please wait up!" instantly, realisation's hand had clenched his hand around Oliver's heart. One thing was left to do, RUNNN.

Whizzing past the scattered runners, he arrived at the station before the ink was dry. Coming to a halt Oliver casually walked towards the ticket station. The organiser had given strict rules not to tell a peep to anyone as news would spread like a wildfire and more people will demand these types of events and he wanted it to be one of a kind.

Impatiently Oliver ignored the long que and brought himself a ticket shunning the vexed people, he was as happy as a queen living in celestial castle. Admiring himself he gave a sly laugh and knew he was going to win this challenge.

On the train

With a spring in his step, Oliver strolled on to the shining train. Sitting at the window seat, he gazed out. He wanted this moment to last for ever as he never thought in his wildest dreams, how picturesque the Mother Earth is. Screech... the train stopped, as if without warning he woke up from his daydream. Startled, he walked unaware of his scenic surroundings. The towering trees danced as the aromatic sensation the cinnamon, cardamom, chilli, and the flavour infused curries. He was so lost in heavenly beauty of nature, that his mission was wiped out of his brain. Taking a deep breath, he spotted a few familiar faces reminding him of his mission. "Oh no! I should have been more attentive. Looks like no chance now," he wept.

"I literally need blood, sweat and tears now. How could I be so absent minded?" From thin air, a crimson dot turned into a ... BUS! He was on cloud nine. The bus ran towards him and he dived into it. Unfortunately, this excitement would not last long. Moaning furiously, the bus devoured every drop of fuel but as the last drop got sucked in....... crash ...bang...kaboom!

He stared down at the map hoping a miracle would happen. A miracle did happen he had sparked an idea. "Dangerous but fast, could this be it?" he wondered. He set off on his journey by leg, on the haunting maze...

20 years later

The smell of coffee wafted into his nostrils as his children pleaded him to tell them a real story of a real hero and he could not stop himself from telling them the story of the youngest winner... and his proud mother couldn't stop smiling.

Honesty is the Best Policy!

By Rahul Maddipatla, Year 3

Once upon a time in a small village called Dharma, there lived two friends named Sid and Tom. Both were poor and used to cut the trees in a nearby forest for their daily earnings.

Tom was a diligent and honest wood cutter. Every morning he woke up early and went out to the forest to cut trees. In the evening he took wood to the nearby village and sold it to earn money. Though he made just enough for his family living, he was so happy and always felt satisfied with his life. But his friend Sid was very lazy, he would sit at home all day sleeping or watching television. He always used to think of making money in easier ways without working hard.

One morning, while Tom was cutting wood near the river bank, his axe slithered out of his hands and fell into the river. For it is the only axe he had, he felt so worried thinking about his daily incomes. He sat near the river bank and cried out loud, "Help me, help me!"

Luckily a wizard who was passing by stopped and asked him "What is the matter?"

Tom replied sadly "I have dropped my axe in the river!"

Looking at Tom, the Wizard thought that he should help him but before he did, he wanted to test how honest Tom was. So, with his magical wand he made a golden axe from the river and asked, "Is this yours?"

Tom stared at it carefully and replied, "No, it doesn't belong to me".

Next, the Wizard got him a silver axe, but again he refused to take it and finally the wizard pulled out the iron axe from the river and asked him "Is this yours?"

Tom happily and with lot of gratitude replied, "Yes!"

The Wizard was pleased with Tom's honesty and gave him all the axes. He thanked the Wizard and excitedly ran back home to tell his wife about what happened to him that day.

In the meantime, his friend Sid was shocked to see him getting rich in one day and while Tom was sharing his story with his parents, he overheard everything.

The next day early in the morning Sid went to the forest to cut the wood near the trees that were on the riverbank and deliberately threw his axe into the river but he did not notice that the Wizard was watching all of this and knew what was going on.

The Wizard walked over to Sid and asked him what happened.

Sid replied, "I have dropped my axe in the river."

The Wizard understood that Sid was cheating but he pretended as though he did not know anything, and with his magical wand he created a golden axe. He showed it to Sid and asked him "Is this your axe?"

As soon as Sid saw the golden axe, he was thrilled and replied, "Yes, this is my axe!"

Then the wizard got furious and said "How dare you lie to me, I know this is not your axe as I was watching you when you were purposely throwing it away into the river. Now you will not get even your own axe back because of your dishonesty!" And the Wizard vanished.

Soon Sid realised his mistake and understood that honesty is the best policy.

The Time Crystal:
Herbajerbs are from Venus

By Jessica Chambers, 9 years old

Thud! Stomp! Thud! Stomp! 10-year-old Ben's feet banged loudly on the smooth coffee coloured floor as he dragged his heavy feet across the Museum. Not even seeing his bored reflection in the polished surface staring back at him was amusing anymore. A twinkle on the floor abruptly caught his eye. He leaned over to seize the strange small, apricot, kite shaped stone which was no bigger than a wedding ring. He pinched it between his fingers to bring it gently and slowly up to his pale face for investigation. Suddenly, a blinding miniscule dot of light appeared in front of his baby blue eyes which were as wide as saucers. His mouth opened but no sound came out, just a silent gasp of amazement.

A whoosh and crackle filled his ears; a blazing neon rainbow erupted from the stone like a spewing volcano coming back to life. The vivid colours of scarlet red, lemon yellow, effervescent emerald, sparkling sapphire, and luminous lilac danced around him. Everyone had paused as still as statues. Motionless. Lifeless. A bubble of panic rose from his toes all the way up to his eyeballs, which were still as wide as saucers. Time had stopped! "What the?" exclaimed Ben, totally befuddled.

Falling into space, Ben heard the 'peep-peep!' of steam engines from an industrial era; the sound of stone age men yelling; dinosaurs roaring and screeching, finally a strange "Gow-oooo-ga" type howl. A wormhole through space and time had swallowed Ben whole!

Ben tentatively opened his eyes and felt the soft tickle of the lush glossy green grass on his skin. He observed the colossal scorching sun shining spectacularly high in the sky; the sun light permeated the wispy clouds with its rays tiptoeing across the utopian landscape. He lay for what felt like hours, but the sun was immovable. He jumped up to his feet so easily he thought he had springs under his shoes! Everything was familiar but this was not home. A noise interrupted his thoughts. As quick as a flash he leapt behind a close-by rock pile, concealing a beautiful babbling brook.

The fish were emerald green and sapphire blue with rose pink stripes along the top, and a violet, snowy striped tail. The fish had one long sharp tooth and a maroon tongue. The fish's eye was as big as a tennis ball and had two wavy antennas which would never be still. Then suddenly, a strange furry creature with skin as orange as a carrot, covered in rose-pink spots and bulging horns on top of his head appeared. It looked directly at Ben, quizzically. "Err...h-hello?" asked Ben nervously.

"Gow-oooo-ga! Welcome to Venus" declared the Herbajerb earnestly (with a friendly smile). Ben felt his jaw hit the floor.

"Sorry, where?! Did you say V-Venus?" uttered Ben, astonished. He could feel the penny drop inside his brain with a quiet 'plop'. He realised this was no hoax. He really was on planet Venus. Ben's thoughts raced through his head as he grappled to make sense where he was and what time he was in. The Venus he knew was a tormented, toxic and tempestuous world with temperatures over 400 degrees Celsius (hmmm toasty huh?!). He pondered what could have happened to turn this paradise into the horrible uninhabitable world he knew. Thoroughly discombobulated by it all, Ben felt disorientated. Why was he here? What did he have to do? How would he get home?

Ben remembered a theory by renowned scientist Dr. Jessica Gent that Venus may have been a goldilocks planet like Earth, but 4.5 billion years ago. Venus is closer to the sun than Earth, so it got too hot and its water evaporated. This meant the rain could not wash the bad gases (like Carbon Dioxide) into the rocks creating a 'greenhouse effect'. "I'll never complain about the rain again!" thought Ben. But Earth was further from the sun, so it did not have to suffer the same fate. Humans could stop global warming if they stopped burning fossil fuels which causes the greenhouse gases on Earth. His adventure felt like a warning of what could happen to Earth if global warming continues.

The Herbajerb signalled to Ben to stroll down the peachy rocky road with him "Come! By the way, my name is Ba-ga-gou....and you are?".

Ben replied "My name is Ben, what are you? I am sorry that was rude. I mean…I am a human from planet Earth. I think I went back in time 4.5 billion years to here"

The Herbajerb scrutinised Ben's face carefully. The Herbajerb seemed as intrigued with Ben as Ben was with him, before stating all matter-of-fact, "I'm a Herbajerb of course. Look! We are already here! You can stay for the year," he gave Ben a broad smile.

Ben suddenly felt an arrow puncture his heart, causing a pain in his chest. He felt heartbroken. He missed his family very much and wanted to return home. He did not tell the Herbajerb because he did not want to be discourteous. Ben entered the dim old dirty room which looked like it had not been cleaned in years (yuk!). In the far corner he could see a dusty old bed with ruby sheets and an area which resembled a kitchen with just a double wooden shelf of food and a navy plastic bucket of water filled to the brim.

He wondered into the bathroom and laid his eyes on a bin filled with old saffron stinky sweet-smelling wee. He turned away rapidly and placed his hands over his mouth to stop the lumpy sick (which was rising from his stomach) from exploding out of his mouth. There was also an old bucket of water. He gradually put his pale hand in to the chilly water which felt like 10 degrees Celsius. Little goose bumps dotted his arm like a rash rising from his hand up to his elbow. Surprisingly, he saw a stone crystal at the bottom of the bucket just like his. Except this crystal was azure like the oceans, 'A water crystal,' he thought.

Ben placed the water crystal in his trouser pocket and brought out the museum time crystal instead. He wiped it with his short, nail bitten thumb gently from left to right and back again like a car windscreen wiper. The portal he had opened earlier appeared with a POP! He shut his eyes and squinted. With a loud slam he travelled through the portal back to the museum. He put the crystal back in his pocket but must have lost the water crystal. He hoped it was in good hands. He realised that there was life on Venus (like Dr. Jessica Gent had said) but it got too hot so he knew that if global warming got any worse, planet Earth would be like Venus, a tormented planet of nightmares.

Everyone around him flashed as white as snow and started to move again (as if the journey was over).

He heard his mum shout "Ben come over here!" and raced straight to her as if nothing had happened. He held her warm peach hand tightly. Ben thought "When I grow up, I'm going to stop global warming so we can all live on planet Earth forever. And I won't complain about the rain either!"

The End!

A Treasure Island

By Arnay Gupta, Year 4

There was once a brother and sister called Max and Alice. Max was thirteen and Alice was eleven. Near the summer holidays, they were told they were going to stay with their cousin whom they had never met. They were told their cousin was twelve. They started chatting.

"He is going to fit in well," shouted Max.

"Or she!" exclaimed Alice.

"Dad is it a girl or a boy?" asked Max.

Dad replied," Boy."

"Ha!" teased Max.

A few weeks later it was time to go. The duo where elated. They packed all their things in maroon and verdant suitcases. One hour later, they ran to the car and set off. Two hours later, Alice and Max were bored, so Alice reached for a pack of cards from her pocket and they started playing.

Soon, they reached their cousins house and knocked on the door. KNOCK KNOCK KNOCK! A tall smart man opened the door.

"Hello," he said.

"Hi," they replied.

"I'm Tom your Uncle and I believe you are Alice and Max," he exclaimed, followed by the family.

Soon dad came with the luggage and whispered a few things. Then we went in. Our cousin, Moz, looked robust. He had a friendly, golden dog called Rusty beside him.

The boy questioned, "Do you want to play with my toys?"

They replied, "We would love to."

Moz and Max had a violent nerf battle but Alice played with her dolls she had brought.

Aunt Ruby said to Moz, "How about you go to the island?"

Alice and Max exclaimed, "ISLAND?!"

Moz owned an island.

"Well you have to go tomorrow, it is too late," quickly added Aunt Ruby.

"Awwwwwwwwwww," Alice cried.

Later it was time for dinner. They had a scrumptious, gargantuan pizza for all of them to gobble up. None of them disliked the food and they went to bed. Moz and Max shared a room and Alice got her own.

In the morning, the three had a delicious breakfast of cold bacon; sausages; eggs and beans forgetting about the island. Moz fed the dog some dog food. Suddenly, Max remembered the island and reminded the others.

Moz whispered, "Let's go now because the sun is shining."

They packed their stuff and ran to the beach with Rusty. They found Moz's maroon petite boat. Moz just remembered they had no food so Max had to sprint all the way home to get some. He came back with a bag full of food. They hopped in and sailed to the island.

Moz and Max took the oars. It took them some time to get there. It was very arduous. When they reached the island, they unloaded the sack. They were all famished and started eating. They all ate club sandwiches. When they were playing, they spotted a map Moz had never seen before. The map showed a secret dungeon with secret ingots in it. They wanted to find the ingots but it was too late so they decided to go back home.

When they reached home Uncle Tom was there with terrible news. He was going bankrupt so he had to sell the island. The children felt melancholy.

Moz was clever and astute, "In how many days are you going to sell it?"

"One week," replied Uncle Tom.

Then Moz thought, they had one week to find the ingots.

They quickly clambered to Moz's room to study the map. It looked like the dungeons were on the left side of the castle.

In the morning they were feeling rapturous. They grabbed food and other things required. Rusty was accompanying them so he could guard them. Rusty was such an outstanding guard.

When they reached the island, they sprinted to the left side of the towering ruined castle. They found the entrance and managed to enter the drab dull dungeon. They filed down the stairs and walked around the dark dungeon.

In the dungeon, they spotted the man who has inquired about purchasing the island (he had seen a gold bar on the island and knew there was more).

"Do you think he wants the gold?" questioned Moz.

The children found the gold but the man stole it from them. Moz had a plan so he told Rusty to act normal. They ran to the shore gasping for breath. Max and Moz kicked the boat until it had a hole. The boat sank.

They hopped their diminutive maroon boat and sailed away. Once their parents knew the succinct, they called the police and told the whole story.

The police sent a ship to the island. The police caught the man and came back with the ingots.

They got the gold and didn't need to sell the island. It was published in the newspaper and everyone was proud of them.

THE END

The Golden Treasure

By Declan McQuillan Woodhouse, 10 years old

Walking along the beach on a sunny Sunday, breathing in the sea air and watching the tide coming in are the reasons why I love coming to Swanage.

While I was looking out to sea something suddenly caught my eye. I walked slowly towards it. I picked it up at the seafront and dusted all the sand off. It looked like a really old bottle, with a cork in the end. Looking closer I saw a piece of rolled up paper in it. It took me a while to open because the brown cork was in it tight. Eventually I did it. I took the piece of paper out feeling worried. It looked like a map, a really old map, with creases in it. It also looked like a treasure map with ~ THE GOLDEN TREASURE ~ written on it. It was a map of Swanage with a big black X marking where the golden treasure was. The X on the map was leading me to Corfe Castle. I was curious what it led too so I decided to follow it.

The quickest way to Corfe Castle was the old steam train. The train station was not too far away, I set off down Shore Road and then turned right onto Station Road and found the station in front of me. I headed into the station and went up to the ticket office to get a ticket to Corfe Castle. I was shocked that it was only £1.60 for a child ticket.

I then headed out onto the open-air platform, luckily for me the old steam train was sitting there waiting to depart, I heard the conductor blow his whistle and shout, "ALL ABOARD!" I quickly got onto the train and found a seat next to the window. With a big jolt and a high-pitched whistle, the train started to move out of the station. As the train pushed on down the tracks gently rocking me from side to side my thoughts turned to the what the treasure might be, could it be a chest full of gold coins and jewels?

When I arrived at Corfe Castle, I stepped out of the train station and looked up the grassy bank in front of me at the ruins of the castle itself sitting imposingly on top of the hill, hoping that the map wasn't going to take me in that direction as it looked really hard work to reach to top. I took out the map to see where I needed to go and luckily it showed the treasure was not at the castle. I walked round all the ruins so I could carry on my journey to that treasure!

The map was leading me to a place called ~ The Blue Pool. I had visited it before but that was a long time ago.

I found a busy bus station with all the people dressed in t-shirts and jeans, all different kinds of ages. They were all standing silent and cramped in the small bus station, but luckily, the bus came. A big, red, bus, saying ~ 35 THE BLUE POOL ~ on it. I hopped on it and realised a child ticket was free! That saved me my spending money! I sat on the leather seat right at the back on the top floor next to a big tough looking man with some headphones on, I could hear the music he was listening to, I was surprised that such a big tough man was listening to Little Mix, but he seemed to be enjoying it.

As I sped along the A351, I saw loads of people enjoying the sun at the camp site, Lenctenbury Farm. Therefore, I knew I would be getting off soon. I pressed the bell and made my way down the stairs, I thanked the driver and got off the bus. Standing at the bus stop I noticed how busy the road was, it took a long time before the bus could edge its way back into the traffic. I took out the map once again, looking for the way go, I headed down Blue Pool Lane which would take me down The Blue Pool, walking down the road I laughed to myself, they couldn't have taken long thinking up the name of this road.

After what seemed hours I finally reached The Blue Pool, once through the car park I found a path which was sign posted to the lake, the path took me through the tall trees of the forest to the lake, looking down the steep clay banks at the beautiful still blue water. I walked over to a map which was on a wooden information board by the path which led around the lake, the map told me that the water was so blue because the light diffracts from the clay suspended in the water, it also told me that I needed to be around the other side of the lake, the X on my map showed me it was the picnic area I needed to go to.

I finally made it to the picnic area and had a careful check around all that was there. After checking all around the white, square-shaped café, I noticed the name of the café… I felt so deflated…the name of the café was The Golden Treasure…ALL THIS TIME I WAS LOOKING FOR A CAFÉ, AND NOT SOMEONE'S BURIED TREASURE.

I sat down at a bench just looking at the map when the waitress came over and said to me, "Oh you've found one of our flyers!"

I looked at her in disbelief as she carried on talking to me.

"These are very rare, I'm so glad you found one! Since you found it, it entitles you to a free fish and chips and a free dessert!"

Tucking into my fish and chips, I thought, this may not be golden treasure that can make me rich, but my tummy thinks that, the cod is golden treasure.

Journeying Through Video Games

By Roshni Syed Rafiq, Year 5

It was a gorgeous day; amber rays splashed onto a number of granite slabs. An array of cotton clouds loomed overhead whilst the sky was coated in a layer of lapis. Down below, was a gravel car park; upon that lay an army of cars. One such car pulling up on the parking lot – an iris one – revved and screeched. Eventually, the noise came to a standstill.

Out of it came a gaunt, surprisingly athletic, tall figure. The main character of the story. Eve. As she did so, she blushed profusely, as most cars were lacey or lapis usually, and iris was an odd car colour. As she hastened away, the car became nothing but a mere dot. Her chestnut mane cascaded behind her, her sapphire-granite eyes widened, as she awaited the fun, her real fifteen year old persona faded away. From her claret trainers, to her navy jeans, to her printed shirt, everything was tingling with anticipation.

Finally, she, along with her mum, dad, seven year old sister, Kate and her five year old sister, Ava, crossed the translucent doors into the ample arcade. Eve blushed with excitement. Before anyone could say, "Wait, you need the money Eve!" she galloped towards one of her favourite games 'Transportation'.

That was when Eve's family chorused, "She hasn't got the money!"

Meanwhile, Eve groaned at having tried multiple times to start the game but ended up fruitless. She thumped her fists on the game angrily. Then, Eve remembered that she forgot the money. Sheepishly, she shrugged her shoulders and darted away.

As Eve darted and her family sprinted, a sound came… A BIG, FAT BANG!!!

Ava, in a bewildered state asked, "Mummy, is big sissy awright?" (Now reader, I can spell 'alright', but Ava needs to learn how to pronounce some words.)

Mum scratched her head and answered, "Yes. She should be up soon. She just banged into us."

Ava peered at Eve, dazed and flat on the floor.

Eve finally awoke, rubbing her head, her dishevelled hair in her weary eyes. "M-M-Mon-Money," she stuttered. "W-W-Whe-Where is it? Money." This was the only word in her head so far.

Mum looked so shocked.

Dad leisurely conversed, "Now Eve, I know you want to play video games but don't you realise what happened? You need to go to a doctor now." Dad was always good at these motivational chats and stuff. If there was an election, then he would have won.

A few minutes later, Eve was on a rolling bed, in a doctor's study. The doctor conveyed, "Nothing to worry about, well that's what's recorded. It's only a matter of time before she can play the games."

Eve's mum burst into tears and implored the doctor with a million thank yous.

Eve smacked her hands on her head as their situation was bad enough. A fifteen year old fainted on the floor! She wouldn't hear the end of it. She needed a 'Dad speech' again. What if a popular girl had seen?

As the iris vehicle departed, she peered out of the window, trying to forget the incident and Kate's constant words, 'Are you ok sissy?' It was an irksome song and scene, playing in her head.

After a space of time, they finally arrived at home. Eve flung off her trainers, trudged upstairs and slumped on her bed. Soon, that whoozy feeling crept over her again. Suddenly, the world was spinning in flat circles and in a second she was in the arcade...

She was bewildered. She wasn't dizzy not tired. What was happening? She was fully awake. She paced her way up to 'Transportations' again, with £5. She inserted it in the machine and played. Wow! She scored a lot of points; more than usual. She crossed Round 11; a round she had never passed.

In a blink of an eye, an iris portal emanated. Just one step. Everything changed. Suddenly, she was seated in an amber carpet, longing to collapse in the arms of a rippling, gurgling, ultramarine body. The beach! Oh no! She slipped out of the moment. Another bunch of tumbling to do! Ugh! Where was she going now? Eve was suspended in sheer raven, deep, deep down...

The World Between the Two Trees

By Imani Egau, 10 years old

Among the clicking of crickets and the lazy humming of bees, the aroma of barbecued food lingered in the air. Laughing and playing, the two girls were catching each other in the blazing hot sun. A few minutes later, the girls were exhausted and sat to have some delicious, mouth-watering, appetizing barbecued food that Betty's father had prepared for them whilst they were playing around in the garden.

After lunch they both went for a wander around the garden. First of all, they went to walk at the end of the garden, which was slightly overgrown.

Unexpectedly, as she crossed the stone path, Cathy accidentally faltered on a pebble as small as a mouse and tumbled over it flinging a small door, about the size of an armchair, wide open which led into a magic portal.

"Look Betty, look what I've found! A door to a magic portal," cried Cathy.

Sprinting, Betty came over from the nearby tree and found that the small coffee coloured door concealed among the fence for years had finally opened and led to a magic portal. Betty squealed with joy as she leaped up and down. Finally, she asked, "Where do you think this portal leads to? Should we go inside?"

"Yeah sure," replied Cathy.

They both held hands and stepped inside . . .

However, this place wasn't ordinary but very queer, there were ebony skies and the trees were joined together like a crowd of vivid jade umbrellas with a spidery tangle of ivy twisted around the trunks. Without warning, Betty trod on a beautiful scroll wrapped around with a scarlet satin ribbon. Cautiously, she picked it up, unwound the ribbon and held it out. In fancy handwriting the scroll read:

Dear Betty and Cathy,

You have come here to save our kingdom from the wicked Wizard. This villain is not an ordinary villain but he has turned our world into a wretched mess. In order to save our kingdom, you must follow these steps:

Up till oak tree, right till bungalow, up till red gem, up till footprints, down till footprints end, up till blue gem, right till bush, right till next bungalow, up till green gem, up to the lair

On the way you will find two unicorns for you to ride and three gems. With these gems you shall put them in the three holes you will find at the Wizard's lair. When you have done this the door will unlock. You will find a golden key and a treasure chest, use the key to open the chest and our world will turn back to normal.

Yours sincerely,

Her Majesty the Queen

P.S. When you have done this the Wizard will lose his power.

Trudging tirelessly, the two girls began their treacherous quest to find the evil Wizard's lair. On the way they came across an ancient oak tree with tangled branches like hair. They both knew for sure that this was one of the landmarks on the letter, both of them turned right and walked on. As they strolled on, they caught a glimpse of an archaic bungalow and walked to it. Behind it they found the most beautiful unicorns in the world one was a glamourous glossy fuchsia and the other was an elegant azure colour.

The girls jumped on, sitting comfortably on their unicorns, preparing for take-off. Soaring through the air, the unicorns were planes gliding in the raven sky. Betty glanced at the jet-black sky where she saw the most radiant, glistening rose gem she had ever seen.

"Look over there, that's the first gem!" called Betty.

Gracefully, they swooped down to pick it up and placed it in Cathy's unicorn's sack. On their laborious quest, they encountered two more, one amethyst and the other lime. The girls could scarcely open their eyes when they found the evil Wizard's lair, a thick cloud of smoke was puffed out of the chimney as the ebony figure danced in the moonlight. By all this the girls knew instantly who this was. Blackener Bert – the wizard . . .

As swiftly as a bird, the unicorns landed on the shamrock grass. Finally, they found the right door and inserted the three gems into the three holes. Instantly, the door was unlocked and inside sat a golden key as still as stone. Cautiously, Cathy reached into the cabinet and took the key, she inserted the key carefully into the lock and opened it . . .

Out came dwarfs, mermaids, trolls and many more creatures of all shapes and sizes. Mermaids laughed and splashed around, trolls jumped and sang and unicorns neighed with joy. Suddenly, the most glamourous man and woman flooded out of the chest hand in hand. Slowly weakening, Blackener Bert eventually vanished.

"We shall crown you the Princesses of Magiccornia!" announced King Phillip and Queen Helen.

"Long live Princess Cathy!" shouted a voice from the crowd.

"Long live Princess Betty!" yelled another.

"And now you must return to your world," declared Queen Helen.

And in a puff of smoke they were gone . . .

"Hello where have you been?" asked Betty's dad suspiciously.

"We've been on an adventure," they replied.

Around the World in 80 Rides

By Mia Bhute, 10 years old

Hi, my name is Mia and I love to cycle. Since the lockdown, every day, I ride my bike up and down my lane, and it is the one thing I look forward to. I also enjoy doing bike tricks and teach my sister Aarya and my brother Rihaan. I taught them tricks like: standing up on their pedals, riding with one free hand and plonking both feet on the frame while the cycle moves forward due to the momentum.

As I was observing how long Aarya could hold a new hand position (while cycling), my bike bumped into a stone and crashed. Luckily, I only grazed my ankle but my bike's tyre valve was damaged.

Heartbroken I trudged indoors and narrated the whole story to my Dad. He reassured me that he'll buy a new valve and teach me how to replace one myself. From despair my expression turned to happiness, but soon I was utterly bored.

Two long days passed with no riding but on Saturday afternoon a package arrived at our doorstep. Buzzing with excitement I took out my bike and swept away the dust, cleared the cobwebs (mostly fictional as it had only been 3 days!!) and brought it out for mending. My Dad and I slowly dismantled the break, loosened the skewer and took the wheel out and set it down. After a lot of screwing and pumping and gliding the job was complete and my bike was as good as new. I thanked my Dad and decided to take it for a spin.

Excited to be back on my bike I zoomed down the lane and turned a corner, but then I noticed this wasn't my lane! Where was the great oak tree or old Rick's home? And the smell of Madeline's muffins vanished.

Then the weirdest thing happened, an auto rickshaw rode past me! On its back was a familiar tri colour flag with the slogan "Horn Please" below it. My heart skipped a beat, was I in India??!! I always wanted to travel the world, so I decided to take a break from worrying and explore further.

I saw valleys of emerald with beautiful houses scattered around. A shimmering lake slapping smooth shiny stones. I wondered, as I looked to the horizon, what breath taking view would come from its zenith. I dashed up.

From the top, I saw a humongous fayre sprawled across the flat valley. I looked up and noticed a colourful sign saying "Village Mela". I bounced into the fayre and felt a tidal wave of delicious smells waft over me (must be the numerous food stalls). I see a variety a multi coloured tents, Mehndi stands, dance performances, carousels, and rides.

I rushed to the food stalls first and tried an Indian sweet named "Gulab Jamun" which tested heavenly. I then swallowed these round savoury balls filled with spicy and sweet sauces and potato chunks called "gol gappas", they were a bit fiery for me. In hindsight I should have tasted them the other way around!

After my stomach was filled to the brim, I found the first seat I could and sat down. A girl, around the same age as me, seated herself next to me. Suddenly, the seat started to move up. I was on a Ferris wheel!! I felt my "gol gappas" rising in my throat, desperate to blast off like missiles. The girl nudged me with her elbow and handed me an orange sweet. I thanked her with my eyes (afraid to open my mouth) and started sucking on it vigorously. All through the ride she told me about her family, friends and her house on the other side of the hill.

Before we knew it, the ride was over and we were almost best friends! We decided to go to the puppet theatre to watch the interesting story of Ramayan, it's a major Sanskrit epic of ancient India where there is victory of good over evil. I was mesmerised by the handiwork of the puppeteer. It was only at the end when I noticed that the sky was darkening, that I told my friend that I needed to go home. I reluctantly hopped onto my bike and rung the bell as a goodbye signal for her. Suddenly everything turned into a swirl of dust and when I brushed the sand out of my eyes, I found myself right next to the great oak near my house!

I parked my cycle in the garage and sauntered thoughtfully to my door. Aarya rushed to open the door with baby Rihaan clapping in delight at my sight, this brought a smile to my face and I was happy to be back home.

After dinner, I narrated my adventures to Aarya and Rihaan and we slept dreaming about the Mela. I had so many questions: I wondered if the magic would work again, will I go to the Mela or someplace new, can I bring Aarya and Rihaan along? Soon sleep took over.

Written for my brother Rihaan Dogra's first birthday, as a gift.

The S Pendant

By Diya Nair, Year 4

A few years ago, my mum and I moved to Italy. We were staying in an old castle that my mum had bought, planning to do it up and convert it into a Bed and Breakfast.

Given that it was a castle I was obviously going to claim the princess room for myself, but what I saw made my heart sink. The walls were painted in what can only be described as a dirty beige, lacking both colour and spirit, and had neither a closet nor a bookshelf. Instead, the only items to be found were a narrow bed and antiquated trunk. It had been a lengthy drive out into the wilderness, and I couldn't recall the last time I saw another living soul. However, I was too exhausted to think about this and jumped onto the bed, plunging into a fitful sleep.

I woke up with a start, mind racing. As I lay in bed trying to work out why, fragments of a dream I just had began to flash in front of my eyes. There was a king in all his regal splendour walking along a hedgerow of white roses and besides him walked the most elegant princess imaginable. She was adorned in a golden gown that had puffed out sleeves and stars on the skirt. Ebony hair rested on her shoulders and tiny earrings peeked out from behind. Around her neck was a choker that had an S-shaped pendant hanging from it.

As dawn broke, I leapt out of bed and made my way downstairs for breakfast.

Upon seeing me, Mum remarked, "You look lively today. Did you have a restful night?"

"Of course," I exclaimed, "I'm going exploring today."

As I wolfed down my breakfast, I stared out at the white roses from the window.

I made a beeline for the roses. I pulled up short, skidding to a stop as I rounded a corner and came face to face with an ivory statue of a king holding hands with a princess wearing an S pendant.

That night, I saw an iron door at the end of the garden with stairs descending into a dimly-lit chamber, a single candle illuminating a full-size portrait of the royal family. My eyes came to rest once more on the now-familiar choker with the now-familiar 'S' pendant.

The next morning, I ran headlong into a drizzle – undeterred, I bounded straight past the statue of the princess and reached a wall of ivy. Dejected and frustrated with this, I aimed a kick at the wall and - BANG – heard the rumble of metal. The faintest glimmer of hope beginning to take root within me, I shoved the ivy aside and opened the door. Almost tripping down the steps, I got to the dimly-lit chamber and my eyes adjusted as I gazed in awe at the painting. I froze, feeling a *presence* and turned around, heart palpitating audibly and breath stuck in my throat, my gaze drawn to the choker with the 'S' pendant...

"Hi, I'm Sofia. Will you be my friend?"

Bobbie and The Ruby Staff of the Pyramid

By Prahen Mahendran, 10 years old

Chapter 1. The Invasion from the Moon

Hello, my name is Bobbie. I live in the UK in my Grandfather James's mansion with my extraordinary parents; my bodacious brothers, Bennie and Gerrie and spectacular sister, Jane; Mrs. Brown, our scientist; Dr Jamie Orchard and the last but not the least, our family-like chauffeur, Randy.

A week ago on an eerie night, I lay snoring loudly in my snug, comfortable bed. This unusual night, I heard a BANG! I felt my ears explode and curiously slipped my fatigued feet into my slippers.

Tiptoeing, I went down the steps. I heard a voice coming from outside.

I took a peep out of the intricate window, which always shone bright. A creature, who had turquoise skin, stood in front of a silver rocket ship and bellowed in a deep echoing voice, "We come from the Moon."

"We've come to conquer the Earth; we, the Moonsters, will be victorious!" he laughed menacingly.

Suddenly, pure, destructive darkness devoured the navy blue sky without mercy...

A deafening silence consumed the city. My heart raced at the speed of light. A cold shiver slipped down my spine. I gulped. I trembled as the ground shook violently. A flood of sticky, slimy sweat covered me.

Many creatures, akin to the first, emerged. They were wielding Lasers shot out from guns. The enormity of this situation was very high.

Still staring out of the window, I noticed an alien Moonster retreating after getting shot by a ray of light. I grinned. An idea sprouted in my brain.

I sped up to my room and grabbed a torch, which shot blazing rays.

I slammed open the door, headed outside and strategically illuminated the incandescent ray precisely on the alien Moonsters. Laughing joyfully, I was allayed. My perfect family, who were standing a few yards away, gazed at the magnificent sight of them departing helplessly.

I felt a sudden impulse to chase after them.

"Boys," Mum began, "It's time to take you to space".

I was overwhelmed! I clambered into our rocket enthusiastically. The engine roared, as Mum started it. Flames spat out from the bottom and we soared into the sky. We flew through the thick atmosphere. Stars twinkled and the moon glowed. We accelerated and chased their rocket close behind.

"Bobbie! Start blasting their cannons," Mummy screamed.

"Gerrie and I are on it," I responded.

"Come on Jane, let's help too." Bennie added.

Bennie and I jumped onto a gargantuan chair. We took the right side and got a clear view out of the transparent glass. Fire beams shot out of our rocket blasting the laser cannons into ash. I grinned. My thumb rapidly pressed the delicate, crimson button. Explosions filled part of space around us. My heart pounded thunderously. Blinking vigourously, my eyes glared at the enemy. I hammered my fists onto the velvet, bright button and a searing flame shot out of the cannon. It charred the rocket and turned the cannons into dust. Scattering into space, it disintegrated into millions of fragments.

" We won!" I exclaimed, flabbergasted. Bliss bubbles popped wildly in my stomach

Chapter 2. The Prophecy

My alarm reverberated, interrupting my serene sleep. Reluctantly, I turned it off like a sluggish sloth. Yawning, I shook my weary eyes open. The sun, that glistened lustrous gold, blinded me causing me to plunge onto the carpet. Dizzy, I tried to insert my feet delicately into my silky, emerald slippers. I departed my room and I suddenly remembered to change my pyjamas into something impeccable. Rummaging through my cupboard, I found some stylish formal clothes.

I slid down the smooth handlebar of our staircase. I sat down in the lounge and stared at the glistening chandelier. A fragrant aroma wafted up to my nose. It tantalized me over to the kitchen. I ventured to the exquisite table, which held the delectable meal. Greedily, I gobbled my serving and noticed Grandfather James wasn't here.

"I FOUND IT!" exclaimed Grandfather James.

The Prophecy that he had rediscovered contained a cryptic riddle. It read "A jewel of red, will be found on a bed, in a land of sand, in a triangle that is grand, the biggest of the trio."

"I think it means a desert in Egypt," I began.

"And I think it means a Ruby on a coffin," continued Bennie.

"And the Pyramid of Giza," Gerrie contributed.

"Very smart!" complimented my daring dad.

Minutes later, we zoomed through the clouds.

Chapter 3. Egypt

As the lustrous, amber sun leaped over the serene horizon in the crisp, cerulean sky, we swirled elegantly in the stratosphere. Jets of steams twirled like a graceful swan.

Sitting next to Randy in the cockpit, my weary eyes started to close and I went into a deep sleep. The flame's roar turned to a crescendo.

"Wake up Bobbie!" the gentle, peaceful voice urged.

My eyes jerked open. It was Jane.

Her sapphire eyes, which were pools of blue oil, sparkled in the light. Her black, silky hair ran down her shoulders. She wore a pink shirt and a crimson skirt.

We shot down and plunged into the golden grains of sand. The pyramid was a thorn that poked the brightness. I approached the oldest of the Seven Wonders of the World. Hieroglyphics were engraved on steady, smooth, strong, sharp stone bricks. I scrutinized it meticulously. I had an authentic khopesh memento, which I used to scrap open a brick.

Now it was clear: *Ruby Staff in the Chamber of Horus.*

I took a step into the room, which was armed with weapons of the gods on the rocky walls. I trudged through the hall and Jane opened a door carefully in order to not break anything. A mysterious chamber held an array of pillars to cross a deep gorge.

Mum touched one and a scorching blaze of fire erupted up to the ceiling- which now had charred patch of black.

A whirring sound of blades slicing the air echoed around the radiant room. I reassured myself as Randy, Mrs. Brown and Jamie were cautiously guarding the emerald plane.

Like a swift cheetah Jane leaped, Dad raced, Mum slid and Gerrie and Bennie sprung towards the ancient artifacts. At that point, I glazed with my mouth wide open and speechless. Unfortunately (for me), I was left to face a cavernous catastrophe. Flames sparked. Water gushed. Wind whipped and lightning struck.

With all my might I slipped through the shards of colourful elements. Exhausted, I stumbled. I had arrived!

"Wrong chamber," Dad discovered.

I groaned with displeasure and moaned with dissatisfaction. Drooping my head down like a dying flower, I trekked to the exit, which felt like it was miles away.

We entered a different chamber. I heard a growl. I stared and saw a beast. Vicious, jagged teeth roamed in his tight jaw. Dishevelled fur swarmed on his body. Its claws were swords as white as fluffy clouds. I screamed and we all fled out.

"Lads, a little help please," requested Grandfather in the last chamber. A gang of black-hooded figures surrounded my family. Randy, Jamie and Mrs. Brown were also cornered. Only Bennie and I barely managed to escape.

"Who are these guys?" I wondered. We ran towards the staff. A muscular man with a huge silky moustache jumped in front of me and I hesitated. Briskly, I drew my sword and defended myself from his barbaric hands.

"Go Bennie!" I yelled at the top of my voice, which felt like it cracked in half.

Bennie drew the staff (which lay before his sharp eyes). A ruby light shone radiantly.

Suddenly out of the blue, the tomb began to crumble.

"Run!" I screamed and ran for my family and my life.

We were freed from its hogging hand, as it crumbled to the ground consuming the villains.

Chapter 4. Part One Complete

The engine hissed and the plane took off. At home, I was shocked that this was only the first jewel weapon out of four.

Grandfather explained, "The three remaining are THE DIAMOND SHIELD OF DEFENCE, THE SWORD OF POWER, and THE GOLDEN SPEAR OF ACCURACY."

"We terrifically found THE RUBY STAFF OF STRENGTH!" exclaimed Joyful Jamie.

I yearned to find the others. I will but later. Now I need to enjoy myself.

An amazing hour later we had a splendid party. The disco ball shone multi-colours. Everyone was superbly dancing, as I sipped an exotic glass of juice. Mocktails of exquisite taste were served on fragile silver platters. Smiles of faces illuminated our majestic mansion.

Oh what a marvellous breath-taking adventure!!!

THE END

Speedoaster vs Tricker

By Sumant Rathi, Year 4

Surprisingly, an 11-year-old boy whose name was Jack, was reading the newspaper. As soon as he flicked the page, his eyes were stuck and glaring at a piece of information. Jack howled for his dad Brian who rushed over to him as he has never heard his howl like that ever in the past.

When Brian had some vision, he could see Jack was pointing to a newspaper article which was in bold. In the corner of Brian's head, he breathed a sigh of sweet relief as Jack wasn't at risk. As soon as Brian got a closer look of the tabloid newspaper, he saw that it said "Reach France without flying and get a prize of £15000."

The article had no more information just a website. As quick as an aeroplane Brian and Jack decided to look it up. They both googled and found out that 95 people had already signed up out of a 100 people.

Jack rushed, "Quickly signup as only 5 spaces are left."

Brian instantly signed the form and a message appeared, "We will contact you in 48 hours, the race will be starting in Central London at 2 o clock 10th June."

As soon as they finished the online enquiry form a BANG came from front door. They opened the door, it was Jack's mum, Lucy. They were delirious with joy to share this news. Eventually Mum found out about it from the beeping messages on Brain's phone. This would be a dream come true if they got to participate in this race. Jack was extremely happy as he loved adventurous activities.

As soon as Jack's twin brother, James, came back from guitar class, the whole family sat around the dining table discussing traveling ideas. The first thing was to get a confirmation from the website and everyone was so furious - what if they didn't get a place in this race? As a family they all decided to get themselves prepared for this adventurous trip even if they weren't selected. Therefore, every one divided the task for getting prepared for this expedition. Jack's job was to find food to eat during the travel James' job was to find out the route with Mum and Brian's job was finding the routes when they reached France. They got on with all the work.

When Lucy came back from work, she rushed over to the mailbox. To her surprise she spotted eccentric post. While she was trying to understand the post, an electricity whizzed through her nerves. She was mortified like a manic. She was nervous but on the other side she was excited because it was the race letter.

The twins spotted mum with a letter so they scurried to mum to grab the letter. Confidence mounted on the twins face as they read the letter. They both high-fived each other and informed their parents about the delightful news.

It was 10th June 2019, the race day had arrived. They were keeping hydrated on the very arid sun-drenched day. Before they started the race, they all got a walkie talkie to keep in contact with the race organisers. Surrounded by strangers and waiting for the sound of the starting pistol, they were all ready and pumped up for the race like a plane about to take off. KABOOM the race had started.

Jack ran as fast as he could to reach to the car, his heart was pumping hard. Mum drifted the car with speed, Brian put the postcode and followed it until they needed refuelling. So, they used the advantage and swapped drivers. Mum could have some rest but she didn't have time too. The family was at the petrol pump for refuelling but mum heard a PSSSSSS sound. She rushed out and saw it was a flat tyre. She knew that it was because of the quickness. They borrowed another car from the petrol pump and drove off like maniacs.

They made it just in time before the Ferry doors were closing. They were the last to enter the ferry with the borrowed car. The journey from Dover to Paris was 1.5 hours. So, they decided to rest and had some supper. They all wondered why the ferry was not stopping and why it was taking way so long. They went to a bar and decided to ask the bartender why it was taking so long to reach Calais- France.

The bartender was a little confused and replied, "This ferry is not going to Calais, it's going to Alabaster Coast."

The family were shocked that in a gaze they took a wrong Ferry. Panicked aroused in all and they started to tremble. The family needed to find a solution to reaching Calais at the earliest.

So, they quickly made a plan and Brian checked on his laptop how long it would take from Alabaster Coast to the Eiffel tower. They weren't happy as it showed at least 2 hours and 40 minutes. Brian quickly went to customer service at Ferry Dock and enquired about any other options or the best route. But unfortunately, they weren't helpful.

The twins came up with a deranged idea of stopping the Ferry at the closest port. They spoke to their parents first, the plan was that James would pretend to be sea sick, which would mean he couldn't travel on sea for more than 2 hours max. Lucy and Brain weren't convinced about this deranged idea but they didn't have any other option.

James immediately acted as if he was in a real pain with sea sickness. Jack and their parents acted panicking and asked for either a doctor or get them to stop at the port. The doctor arrived at the scene but this didn't help with James fake acting. The ferry's captain had to forcefully stop the ferry at the nearest port which was very close to Calais Port. Brain did all the formalities for checking out from the ferry and they drove out from the ferry like a rocket.

It was 8 in the evening and the family was on the road to Eiffel Tower. It was a breezy evening with a wonderful tangerine sunset. The traffic was moderate but all of a sudden there was a road diversion sign on the road which led to the Eiffel Tower. Brian stopped the car with a screech and he was puzzled. Lucy woke up with this jerk and it didn't take a second for her to understand the trick behind it. She remembered that in France the road diversion is written in red but this one was written in yellow. She immediately asked Brian to disregard this diversion sign and drive pass it.

Brian did as instructed and they were all now becoming worried. The twins saw a familiar car and it was parked after a diversion sign turning. They tried to peep inside the car and found one of the participants was having a snooze. It didn't take long for them to understand that the diversion was definitely a trick to make them loose the competition.

Brian now drove as fast as he could to reach the Eiffel Tower. As Lucy opened the window, she saw that they are being followed by another participant. Lucy had an idea, she requested Brian take a left turn and go straight with a speed and turn again. Brain did as instructed and the twins were updating how far the other cars were. This was becoming really serious but they had to win without fail.

The twins screeched in happiness as they could now see the Eiffel Tower from the car window. The GPS showed they were literally about 0.4 miles away. Other cars were speeding up their gears and this was really getting stern. One of the cars lost their control and this created an accident.

Luckily the twins car just passed that road. The twins called their car "Speedoaster" and the other car which was very close to them they referred to as "Tricker". So Tricker was coming very close of reaching point and Speedoaster were trying their best to beat it.

Brian immediately changed the gear to 6 and just before the touching line speedoaster made it before Tricker. Everyone was now cheering for "Speedoaster". This was like a fantasy fulfilled and they couldn't believe that they had won this competition.

A goofy grin spread across the twins' cheeks. The atmosphere was overwhelming with rays of light bursting through the fireworks. Despite all the hurdles and adventures, finally they had won the most awaited prize. Now they could have a lovely time in France.

The House

By Andrew Popescu, 11 years old

Number 10, Rose Garden Street was known for its eerie appearance, the eeriest on the street. Legend has it, that the bottomless pit is in that very house. Green ivy engulfed the entire front balcony like trailing fingers hanging on for their dear life. It is believed that the tortured souls of previous occupants roam the dark, gloomy corridors within. All you could hear at night were deafening screeches because of them. There were rumours of friends going into the house but not out again. Myself (Jordan), Luke, Abbey and Elena just had to go inside. So we decided to make a plan.

The day came. We stood in front of the towering gate that was ten feet tall - it had deadly spikes with what seemed to be blood on top. Huh, so this was number 10 Rose Garden Street? We cautiously pushed the gate open as it let out an ear-splitting shriek that made us all twitch. Crumbling beneath our feet was dry, disintegrating dirt which vaguely made a pathway. Once our sense of hearing came back to us, one by one, we reluctantly crept towards the front door. Suddenly, the door opened ajar, ushering us in.

Elena carefully pushed it open fully and quickly cupped her hands over her ears. We did the same but this time the door did not creak.

Luke's legs wobbled more than jelly; his forehead was covered in sweat. He squealed expecting something to be behind the door.

"Shhhhh," we all hissed at him. There was nothing there. We cautiously stepped inside. The wooden floorboard underneath my feet let out a high-pitched groan. As we all stepped inside, the door slammed shut behind us. *Strong wind today,* I thought.

That was until Abbey tugged at the door and shook her head in disbelief. The door was locked. The room was now pitch-black, so we tried to look for a light source. Fortunately, I found a switch and without hesitation, I flicked the switch on. Surprisingly, a faint light flickered on.

I sighed in relief but that all changed when a human-shaped silhouette limped from the shadows. It had chains around its legs, hands and neck; stone eyes that pierced through your soul and holes that went from his chest through his heart and back out again. The creature trudged towards me as I stepped back and screamed...

The wooden floorboards cracked under my weight. Suddenly, I fell through them as splinters entered my mouth. They felt like razor-sharp daggers sharpened by the devil himself, forged for murdering. The hole was as infinitely deep as it was terrifying. The last thing I heard was Luke screaming.

Now, the silhouette was chasing Luke into the kitchen but after it realised that Luke was faster, it lost interest in him. The girls split up, Elena went to the bathroom and Abbey went to the living room. The silhouette disappeared as I fell to the ground. I was back at the front door! It must have been an illusion. Even stranger, my friends were there too. We all stepped back in disbelief. We were speechless. Nobody did anything. It was like we were afraid to even breath. It seemed that the 'thing' that attacked us was one of the previous occupants. Does that mean the house is really haunted? I guess we will never really know.

"Jordan! Rise and shine," said my mum, "Your friends are waiting for you."

I put some clothes on and rushed down the stairs. "Hi guys. We are still going to the park right?" I said. The park was a code name for the House on Rose 10 Garden, like museum was the code name for cinema.

"Yes." Luke said.

As we approached the house and stood in front of the towering gate it was just like my dream…

The Tommies Dark Side

By Aaryan Goyal, 11 years old

Bullets ricocheted... happiness collapsed... Germany gasped.

I ran, as fast as my fear could reach. I ran and suddenly jumped into exploding blackness. Had I reached the trenches?

The next morning, I woke up to a wet head. Feeling it made me realise it was sticky. Blood! I got up and hastily rushed to the medical post. I was treated and was back on duty. Grasping onto my rifle, we pushed on. It was then it happened... The Tommie had unleashed it. Gas!

A swarm of fog immediately made us put our gas masks on. Some people hadn't managed to put their masks on in time and collapsed. Right in front of my eyes, men bleeding. Men vomiting violently. Men dying!

Suddenly a rope of bullets obliterated our frontline men. They collapsed like skittles being smashed. We still drove on; shooting our every last bullet. Blood was pouring and men were lying on the ground. The Germans were losing. The Tommies were winning.

Echoing bullets filled my ears, blasting my ear drums. I felt an ache in my heart and then suddenly blackness...

It had all started when I was in the town of Nuremburg, eating a sandwich. My older brother, Heinrich, was playing with his British action figures. Suddenly, a Brobdingnagian bomb approached view. The air raid sirens went off and we covered ourselves in a shelter.

As we clambered out of our shelter, a horror obstructed my view. It was like crumbled foliage. The town had been shattered into shreds. It was then I filled in my soldier application form.

I held my rifle up high and my spirit was jubilant. "Come on Germans! Let's take the Tommies down!"

Trapped

By Riya Goyal, 9 years old

"Let me out of here." Darkness filled the air that surrounded me. "Let me out." The acrid-smelling chemical was slowly rising to my waist. "Let me out." I could only hear myself screaming and wailing. "Let me out!"

It had all started with a drowsy headache. It was always the same, a crushing pain just on one side of my head that came and went in a pattern. Within a couple of days, my loving mum took me for an appointment at the doctor's surgery.

As we came out of the surgery, bizarrely my mum started weeping heavily and that was when I found out... I had shrinkillitis!!

Shrinkillitis is an incurable disease that gives you throbbing and painful headaches and within weeks of developing it, the disease shrinks your body to half the size of a wine bottle. The disease is contagious and spreads by touch. Nobody knew what to do.

As stated, within weeks I had gradually shrunk to half the size of a bottle and now I was in my own ward, self-isolating. Still, nobody knew what to do with me.

So that was how I spent my childhood, stuck in a hospital ward. I attended an online school and my meals were delivered to me each day. I didn't develop any social skills.

Well, my life was going okay until one of the nurses started getting symptoms of the disease too. That was when they decided what to do...

They had to destroy my infectious miniscule body, so they trapped me in a tight-neck bottle with a dangerous chemical inside to gradually finish the job. "Let me out!"

Deep Dark Death

(Narrative of The Highwayman Poem by Alfred Noyes)

By Bisam Kaur

Clatter! Clash! Cling!

"What a racket," thought Tim to himself as he gently groomed and cared for the loyal, chestnut horses. He peeked, like a naughty pixie, and looked at the bright, night moon. The gentle breeze tickled his face like invisible fingers. He could hear the swoosh of the wind and rustle of the leaves.

There were wispy clouds floating carelessly like balls of cotton wool soaring high in the dark night sky. There were shimmering, sparkling stars glittering whilst the moon was shining brighter than the sun. There was a wooden, grimy stable that was set in the courtyard of the inn. It was dark, dirty and dusty; the stable wood could grate anyone's skin like rough concrete. Inside the stable, you could smell the horse's strong stench like the dark, offensive, musty odour of rotten milk.

Tim's inquisitive nose was like a meddlesome creature, so he glanced at the handsome, audacious Highwayman. He was used to taking orders: his tone was husky and low. His face was poker-faced and deadpan, but inwardly he was fighting to remain composed on seeing the Highwayman. Tim was stunned by the Highwayman's attitude and muscular body, but after a minute or two forgot all about that.

 Subsequently the Highwayman crossed the courtyard and galloped gracefully to the old inn. There stood a majestic, three-storey inn, framed with elaborately carved, black shutters. Additionally, there was a low, ancient-looking door with a large brass handle. The inn was enclosed by a metal, elegant gate as if it was trapped and wanting to be freed. The red-tiled roof, with a murky smoke-filled chimney, blew gusts of misty smoke from the trapped cage.

When Tim again peeped, he noticed that the Highwayman was drumming his whip on the window while whistling a merry tune. His whip went THUD, THUD, THUD! like a professional drummer's music. However, peculiar thoughts were whizzing in Tim's mind like, 'I wonder what the Highwayman's doing?' or 'Maybe I should spy on him'. Well, let me tell you, he was spying. Definitely!

So, the next thing he saw broke his heart (because he loved Bess). That so-called burglar was beginning to get Bess's attention and she was flirting with him! In that moment, his inky-blue heartbroken crestfallen eyes reflected his heart's condition on seeing Bess dallying with the Highwayman. His heart split into crumbs as tears streamed from his eyes and cascaded down his cheeks like a waterfall. Anguish tightened around his chest like a savage snake, as despair dug deep inside his heart.

But still, he carried on listening and overheard the Highwayman's scheme, to steal a mountain of gold, earned by an incredulously rich man. With tears in his eyes, he distressfully glanced at Bess, who was giving the Highwayman a true love kiss on his scarlet cheeks as the kiss glistened in the Highwayman's heart.

Once the highwayman left, he was burning with anger and jealousy. But do you readers realise how different Tim was to the Highwayman? Unlike the Highwayman, Tim had a slim body with bony arms and legs. His cheeks were pallid and hollow; and the face flesh was wrinkled and sagging. His creased, unshaven face with blue, deep, mysterious, narrow eyes were hidden beneath a pair of bushy heavy eyebrows. He had a narrow mouth and thin pursed lips concealing two jagged rows of hideous yellow teeth. He had a large hooked nose with narrow, pinched nostrils. His big droopy ears protruding on either side of his head, were obscured by his shaggy straw-coloured scruffy hair as if a bomb had landed on his head. His hands were mucky and grubby; and his nails were chipped and encrusted with dirt and horses' grime.

He looked like a tramp in his lengthy, ripped, shapeless cotton t-shirt that hung loosely on his hips. He wore baggy, beige, battered bottoms. His clothes looked crumpled and faded (more like rags). When he moved, he was like a figure carved from stone. He had a devious crafty gaze and had an empty smile like a carcass.

In a torrent of rage, he came up with a very hideous strategy, he stormed off in a huff to inform the King's guards about the rebellious plot of embezzlement of the Highwayman. Why? Obviously, he wasn't man enough to fight tooth and claw with the Highwayman so decided to butter his bread on both sides instead.

In a short period of time, he observed the guards' presence and watched as they positioned themselves in a tactical technique, in order to be rough and ready to confront the Highwayman. Astonishingly, to Tim's surprise, the guards tethered Bess and put her at death's door by placing a gun to her chest in order to use her as a bait for the Highwayman. Seeing this, he got despondent and his eyes turned blurry to create a misty cloud of lonely fog.

Meanwhile, the Highwayman gradually made his way to the inn, when he heard a thunderous BOOM and a familiar shrill scream coming from the inn. He leapt at the reins of chestnut brown horse and rapidly dashed to the inn like a cheetah. He heard a blaring BANG, which sounded like a booming gunshot. He turned and discerned Bess, lifeless and motionless: blood cascading from head to toe. It was a blood-curding, hair-standing, spine-chilling moment for Tim.

With sorrow surrounding him, he noticed that the guards slowly strode to confront the Highwayman. He witnessed the guards shoot the Highwayman dead on the spot, so he looked like a listless statue. He received his remuneration from the guards, because he had disclosed them about the Highwayman's scheme. He was both; elated for the reward but more depressed about the murders, - especially Bess's. He departed back to the dark inn, blubbing all the way to his dwelling, with thoughts of slayings for his company. Was it worth it?

The Dangerous Journey

By Ane Jekabson, 10 years old

One morning, a young 10 year old girl named Stephanie, woke up to find 2 people sitting in her room. There was a woman and a man. The woman was skinny, had long brown chestnut hair, sky blue eyes and freckles on her cheeks. She wore a jumper with a map of the solar system on it, and a long skirt down to her ankles with all kinds of stars over it.

The man, on the other hand, looked like he was a business man. Straight blonde hair, grey suit and shiny black shoes.

"Who are you? What are your names, and what are you doing in my room?" said Stephanie.

"One," said the woman, "My name is Molly, and two, we're going to take you to the International Space Station and-oh yeah, I forgot, his name is Eric," said the woman.

Stephanie froze in both shock, and terrible happiness. She soon found herself dressing up and heading outdoors, toward the rocket launch. It was only then, that Stephanie realised that she hadn't had any training to go into space. She told Molly, but Molly said it was alright and the Stephanie didn't need training for this particular mission.

The three of them got into their 3 pound weight space suits, and crawled into the giant space ship and waited for the launch. Then it was finally time to go to space.

About 10 minutes after launching, Stephanie, Molly and Eric were in space, going exactly to the right place at exactly the right speed. Suddenly, out of nowhere, an asteroid hit the rocket as hard as 100 giant metal hammers!

"GET OUT! GET OUT!" screamed Molly in fright. The two adults and the child crawled out of the rocket through the emergency door which, Stephanie thought, was the smallest door ever. Both Molly and Eric clung onto Stephanie so that she wouldn't float away. The Sun was smiling, but they still felt worried.

After 3 minutes, Stephanie spotted the ISS coming their way. Stephanie knew that it went quite fast, but she didn't think it would be so fast. Without noticing it, Molly pushed Stephanie towards the ISS and then held onto her as she was floating up. Someone inside must have noticed, because some sort of round room started to form and there was a small hole for the 3 of them to get in. When they got in the round room, the hole closed, and the hatch that went inside the space station opened. They floated inside, and took off their space suits that were now weightless.

They spent the rest of the year, working and having loads of fun in space. But little did they know that their troubles were just beginning.

The Invisible Guest

By Sreehari Anoop, Year 5

Kaira slammed the door shut. A man loitered around the doorway that was full of repulsive rats skittering around his legs. Could it possibly be? She broke a bucket of sweat. How could she let him in? He was a stranger and thy Lord did not trust strangers, especially ones in hooded jackets with masked faces. He looked like a cold-blooded MURDERER!

She opened the door a fraction of an inch. She fretted. Click. Lights off. Click. Lights on. What on godly earth was that? The man literally seemed like he had disappeared into thin air. Every nook and cranny seemed exactly the same, but there was more than meets the eye...

In all the syzygies and galaxies in the world, the Lord had chosen him. She crept closer, only to cast her sight upon crimson blood and a fluffy corpse. Her cat! It was slaughtered, macheted and chopped in every way possible. It was so grim, so grisly, that one (especially at the age of Kaira, who was sixteen and hugely timid) could not describe it in proper words. Just as Kaira was about to scream her vocal cords off, there was a knock at the door.

Was God frowning at her right now? No. He was punching her in the face. She saw he had a knife, absolutely smothered with blood, and she was more than ready to BREAK DOWN. So, she sank to her knees and wailed, then trudged up the stairs. The thunder cackled at her plight. If only that man knew what was coming to him!!

When she came back from her fit, the man was nowhere to be seen. She looked down at her knees, and the man was dead. A knock came from the door and Kaira smiled devilishly. Her.. next.. victim.. was.. here!!

The Toy Box

By Hasini Vangapalli, 9 years old

Gazing at the picturesque view, I glimpsed pearl, fluffy, cotton candy clouds careering across the azure sky. The sunshine's rays kissed the clouds making them blush. The aquamarine bushes of trees swayed and waved. The tawny trees stood up proud and tall. They were as majestic as a king and as lofty as a giant. The wind was a thunderous growl like a grizzly bear.

Hi! I am silly Scooby. Well that is what they call me. You will be thinking how can I ramble even though I am a toy? Well I can explain. All the toys in this room can communicate and plod as we originate from Toy World. Over there all toys can speak. Then we were bought by a person named Toby.

Right now, we are trying to get out of this suffocating box. We're searching for something to get us out of this place. There were toys and toys until we found a rusty, relic wedge.

Finally, after an eternity we managed to open the box using the wedge but to our surprise, Toby our owner was in the room. At last we were liberated rather than being held in captivity. We are treated rudely by our owner but our former owner was loving and caring. Toby spotted us. The problem was humans shouldn't know we can talk or move.

Toby bolted down to her mum screaming, "Mummy! Mummy!"

"What is it sweetie pie? Is there an insect or what? You are screaming like some lunatic."

"Theresss..."

"There's what?"

"Thhee... toys were moving and talking."

"Impossible. Let me see." Mum pulled down her spectacles and put her arms on her hip.

Toby and mum sprinted up the winding, everlasting stairs. While all this happened, the toys got into their initial places and decided on a plan. Whispering and muttering between themselves unaware that Toby and her mum were in the room.

Toby opened the box and to her mum's amazement the toys were moving and talking.

"I thought you were lying all along!" exclaimed mum.

"I told you Ma."

At that instant they locked the box tight and chucked it in the car. Speeding, they drove off to the toy shop.

The wind was howling like a frenzied wolf. The clouds cried. The angry monster had woken up. Stamping and roaring like a raven. Crows croak calls while cacophonies echoed crazily and carelessly. CRASH! BASH! BANG!

They arrived at the shop and asked to speak to the manager.

"The toys were moving and talking," barked Toby's mum.

"Umm… I can guarantee you a 100% that the toys are not moving nor talking. That is impossible. We don't sell products which can communicate like a human. That is false marketing. I really think that no one can make that happen in the world."

Toby's mum argued, "But I witnessed it with my own eyes. I WANT A FULL REFUND!" raged her mum.

"Sorry mam. I can't give a refund without a receipt. Plus, the toys have been used."

Toby's mum was exasperated and drove to the garbage centre. She wasn't sympathetic and threw the box in the bin.

What would be our fate?

The Tunnel

By Shenul De Silva, Year 5

Wildly, Billy waved at me across the hill with both arms. I waved back, a huge grin on my face. Then suddenly, the ground gave away. . . The stony-grey clouds danced miserably in the sky. Thunder shrieked as the tempestuous wind whistled. It was as loud as meteors crashing on to the ground.

I observed Billy quivering in fear. "Billy are you alright?" I screamed apprehensively.

"Yes," he answered as he hid behind the lifeless tree. I knew he was not alright as his hands trembled rapidly.

I dashed to Billy. Tears trickled down his ruby-red cheeks as he was crouching for safety. The relentless march of time ticked-on as rain struck down on to the anxious ground. Abruptly, I hesitated. At the bottom of the field, was an ebony-black tunnel. The deafening noise of thunder surrounded the colossal field. Billy and I darted to the pitch-black tunnel.

We had entered. Above us felt like bullets striking down. The petrifying tunnel lead into darkness. Cold sweat dripped down my face. Billy's body shivered. His legs quivered. We strolled together as our eyes scanned around the cylinder-shaped tunnel.

There was mucky mud scattered around the walls. A minute stream of filthy water raced down the entrance. Billy's crystal, clear, snowy white teeth shattered as he crept as slow as a snail slithering across a slimy floor. I paused – Grandma gave me a torch for my birthday! I maintained it in my pocket.

"Phew," Billy claimed as he wiped of the sweat on his forehead. The amber-yellow light glistened as we sauntered further. Not a speck of fear appeared on our faces.

Perpetually, we rambled as boredom wafted in the tunnel. In a split second, growling echoed in the distance. Billy and I froze. This was not the end. . .

We staggered as our legs shuddered. Fear gripped my beating heart as the growling enclosed the area. The magnificent shadow came towards us. The deafening silence made mine and Billy's arms vibrate. The ground began to shake like it was an earthquake. In a blink of an eye, we discovered the monster – it was a bear!

"Ahhhhh! "we yelled as we hastened beneath the boisterous bear and bolted directly away. The malicious monster howled as he stumped towards us. Out of nowhere there were two ways. We decided to go the diagonal way. Silently we concealed at the side of the wall.

At the speed of light, the beast sprinted in the direction we arrived but was not cautious of his surroundings. So, we crawled the straightforward way and finally reached outside. Now the great ball of fire gleamed on us and olive-green leaves muttered joyfully. We travelled our way back home.

But I wonder, where did the bear go?

Trapped

By Riya Shah, 11 years old

"Is she in there?"

"Yes boss!" a muffled voice replied casually. "Forget she ever existed because she never did…"

"Stop joking around!" the 'boss' replied angrily. "Make sure the builders come and start renovating in an hour."

"Wha…What?!" I exclaimed drowsily in shock, as I woke up from an unpleasant dream about being trapped in a cellar alive. I was in an uncomfortable place lying down. Darkness covered the room with its monstrous body. A few of my hundreds of phobias and allergies started to kick in. Terrifying coughs and fits of sneezes all thanks to the dust.

As I attempted to stand on my feet, I banged my head with a deafening thud, slowly losing consciousness once again. My brain unable to grasp its surroundings. As I slipped out of my senses, I noticed the ceiling was caved in towards my puny 15-year-old body…

3 hours later

I pulled myself up gradually, careful to dodge the roof. In a few seconds I became aware of my environment, my heart pounding at the speed of a cheetah. A wave of panic hit me. Now I realised, I was in a miniature space, with just about enough room for one person. My nightmares turning into reality faster than I could breath. Spiders crawling around and ants creeping up my legs. I thumped loudly on the walls, keeping my fingers crossed that someone would hear my pleads.

Sweat beads trickled down my forehead, I knew deep down that I could not survive this living nightmare. Yet, I worked like a maniac to find a way to escape my incoming doom. My phobias took the better of me, my blood pressure zoomed up. I started shivering with fear, and drifted away from reality.

No, I had to keep firm! So, I crawled like a caterpillar to explore this hallucination. The harder I looked for an escape, the more I felt defeated. The cellar was smeared in green mould, threatening to clasp me in its merciless arms. I felt more trapped than ever. Ancient, wooden panelling was above me, they looked like they would rip apart. But… then a crash above me shocked the wits out of me and a surge of hope escaped out of me. With all the strength I had, I punched the walls one last time. Strings of inaudible voices started to seal any exits, burying me alive. My body paralysed…

Bang! Bang! My life slipped away without another word…

Checkmate

By Shnaya Singh, Year 5

The rain thundered, each drop flung down to the ground, as if a floodgate had opened in the heavens above.

Fourteen-year-old Lyra Henderson sighed as she stared at the pelting raindrops. She and her thirteen-year-old brother, Jack, were grudgingly locked indoors on a Sunday afternoon of their "summer" holiday. Broken out of her reverie, she heard Jack calling for her. She hurried over to the door to see what was the matter.

"Look!" he exclaimed. Lyra took a moment to take in what she saw. He was holding an ancient, wooden chess set. The unusual thing was that it emitted a faint, iridescent light that formed a ring around its edges.

"I found it in Nana's wardrobe while foraging for something interesting," he grinned, "Care to have a game?"

Lyra nodded, thrilled. They eagerly unclasped and lifted the lid. Inside, a perfectly ordinary pack of chess pieces and a checked chessboard sat surrounded by a thick coating of dust. The squares were olive green and ecru, matching the ivory pieces. The wood was scratched sporadically with two chipped kings and queens, a shadow of their former glory. The edge was intricately carved into an elaborate pattern of swirls and twirls.

Soon Jack was racking his brain, searching for a novel strategy to execute. Ten minutes into the game and he was in a sticky situation already, with most of his pawns and bishops sacrificed to the opposition. The two were so engrossed in their game that they didn't notice the eerie glow that trapped them, gently enveloping the surroundings. While Lyra was capturing Jack's knight, she began to feel smaller! To her horror, it wasn't her, the pieces were growing bigger by the minute!

In no time, they were towering above Lyra who was tall for her age. The royals and their armies flickered open their eyes.

With that, the queen spoke with authority, "Let the game commence!"

Lyra was dragged to the black team, Jack to the white. The king announced that the triumphant side would shrink to normal size, even the prisoners of war. No such luck for the side conceding defeat, Lyra and Jack were the battalion leaders. The siblings had to rise to the occasion, they couldn't even afford to stay dumbstruck with the goings-on.

Lyra stole a fleeting moment with her brother and lowering her voice by a half octave, whispered, "You win first."

Jack started planning every move. "King," he ordered, "Shift one square right." Then Lyra turned to her king and commanded him to `move one place forward` in order to deliberately jeopardize her side.

It was CHECKMATE! The Ivories were victorious! They astonishingly shrunk as swiftly as they had grown. Now that she had gotten her brother out, Lyra had to extricate herself from this nightmare. Suddenly, she had a brainwave. The glow had to be the source of the magic; she must break the ring force! This was her only choice. She marched her team right off the squares and through the glow, onto the rug under the board. Instantly, the Ravens contracted.

"Yes!" she cheered, her two jewels glistening with joy and fun. She had succeeded in breaking the spell.

Filled with relief, the siblings slumped to the bean bags. They stared at each other in disbelief. The two still couldn't take in their occult experience.

"Next time, no interfering with Nana's ancient artefacts," Lyra lovingly rebuked her brother. "You know she's an archaeologist with heaps of queer objects in her collection!"

Ensuring that Mother, Father and Nana were out of sight and hearing, they gently and leerily placed the box back in the wardrobe. Jack had carefully packed everything in their respective positions. Or so they thought...

In the darkness of the wardrobe, thirty-two pairs of eyes flickered back to life once more.

GAME OVER

Hermione and Hydra

By Emma Giol Butnaru, 11 years old

Many years ago, in a small house in Athens, lived a humble family who worked hard for every penny. After spending most of her childhood at home doing nothing, the youngest daughter, Hermione, decided she wanted an adventure. The perfect chance arose when The Hydra – a five headed snake – would attack the village every week and would take a child.

Eventually, the elders had had enough, so they called a meeting and Hermione immediately offered to go and kill the vicious reptile. Her parents and siblings begged her not to go (as she was but a child herself), but Hermione insisted that she must. As she set off, she looked back at the beautiful village she was leaving behind and thought about what could possibly lie ahead.

After walking for a week, Hermione had reached the woods where the Hydra's lair was rumoured to be. She plodded through heavy rain, almost wishing she were back at home, when suddenly, she felt a sharp tap on her shoulder. She spun around in shock, almost falling over! She could not believe that there was someone else in this seemingly desolate place. Behind her was a ragged, ancient-looking old woman. The woman smiled a crooked smile as she fell onto her knees.

"Oh, sweet saviour?" she screeched. 'Oh, darling child!"

"U...U...Um?" spluttered Hermione, "I am not saviour!"

"Of course, you are!" yelled the woman as she reached into the pocket of her thin, black cloak. "You have come to kill the Hydra!"

As she pulled something out of her pocket, she grasped Hermione's hand.

"Look after this!" she whispered urgently, before disappearing into a puff of smoke.

When Hermione recovered from the shock, she peered into her hands to see a precious red gem (which was probably a ruby) with a golden rim. With a confused raise of her eyebrows, she continued on her journey.

As nightfall approached, Hermione grew hopeless, as she had not found anything. Just then, she tripped over something hard and cold. When she looked down, she saw a small, metal handle. She pulled on it sharply to reveal a narrow, circular hole. In the hole, there was a rotting staircase that looked as though it meandered for miles. Tentatively, she made her way into the depths below.

Eventually, her feet reached firm ground. With only one glance, she immediately knew that she was in a damp, dark cave. She heard a crunch beneath her feet and, fearing for what she would find, she looked down.

Below her foot, was a human skeleton. She hoped this was not a harbinger of what would happen to her. Suddenly, a sharp hiss echoed around the cave. She whipped around and behind her there was a large, five-headed snake. The Hydra. It gave her a belligerent stare as its tongues flicked in and out of its gigantic mouths. The beast was much larger than Hermione had expected. As she turned to run away, she felt a pain in her head as she was knocked onto her knees. The Hydra had hit her on the head with its tail! She fell onto her back, her heart pounding with fear. Staring menacingly, the Hydra loomed above her. The beast's teeth were gleaming, its tail was flicking. This was the end!

Hermione knew that she must not give up. If she could not kill the beast, who would? Bravely, she stared the beast directly into its middle set of eyes and made a shocking realisation. On the Hydra's forehead, there was a gem identical to the one Hermione had been given. In one last attempt to kill the beast, she took the gem out of her pocket and tossed it at the Hydra's forehead. In a blinding flash of light, she saw the Hydra rise into the air and then fall onto the ground with a loud thud. The Hydra gave a furious hiss as it began to shrink, until it was the size of a mere apple. With a pop, it became something else entirely. The Hydra had become a gem!

Slipping the priceless gem into her pocket, she set off back home. Smiling to herself, she thought about Hydra being defeated, she thought about how she had been brave and determined. With this weight off her shoulders, the journey home felt like a breeze.

When Hermione returned home, she held up the gem for all to see. A cheer erupted from the crowd that was awaiting her arrival as her parents and siblings ran to embrace her. The elders gave her family a lot of money, so they were no longer poor, and a statue of Hermione was put up in the town square.

She had many more adventures, but after each one she would return to Athens, which was now a happy place.

The Race

By Vihaan Mohan, 8 years old

Chapter 1

"WANHAHA!" came a voice from Weeping Wally. Because Impertinent Isaac had punched him! 10 minutes later, the race was about to begin. As a speedy vehicle sped past him, some sort of liquid splashed on Sarcastic Steve's backpack.

Finally, after 5 minutes Wally stopped crying. Now, even Non-Frightened Nathan was getting edgy.

In a monotonous tone, a man wearing a blue T-shirt, with blonde hair, and tight grey jeans, stood on the prolonged foot path next to the bumpiest road ever.

After they had all done what the man said, which was to get in their starting positions, he said "Tricked you, there is still 20 minutes to go."

Then everyone said "What was that for?"

Except Sarcastic Steve who started clapping and saying "Well done!"

Chapter 2

Slowly, time faded out and it was almost time. Steve took a deep breath and promised himself that he would not be sarcastic from now on, till the race ended. Also, he simply had to win. Steve then breathed out. As soon as he breathed out, Forgetful Frank threw on Steve forgetting his big moment.

"Ow!" Steve screamed remembering about his promise. 5 minutes later, the race was about to begin, as everyone was getting ready for their eardrums to almost break with the pistol noise, Non-Frightened Nathan was eating sweets.

15 minutes later, the same man came and said "Starting positions everybody!"

Everybody knew he meant it this time so they got into their starting positions. "KABOOM!" the pistol had fired, everybody closed their ears (except Non Frightened Nathan)

Chapter 3

Consigned to oblivion, Steve started scampering really instantaneously to a bus stop, thinking he was in the groove (which he was). The bus was already right there like it was waiting for him! When he got next to the bus the doors didn't open. Steve was perplexed. Slowly, he scanned for the front of the bus. "What?!" Wailed Steve. It *was* out of order, as his smile wore away it was restored with tears. He was thinking how was he ever going to get to India if he already had a problem?

"Calm down," he said composedly. It was time for plan B, the only dilemma was he had no plan B. He sped to look at his map as he could see his competitors in the scope ahead of him. Unanticipatedly, he got the culminating idea.

His idea was very acceptable because there was barely water and barely moving countries, Steve looked at his insignificant map (it was insignificant because it was so small, and plain). Steve had decided to do this challenge as he wanted to check how far he could survive. He was already famous and known as the 'rich coder kid'. Anyway, the plan was to travel across the Arctic Ocean, then to reach Russia, next analyse Mongolia, hunt for China and finally reach India. So on his phone he booked a boat.

Two days later, Steve found himself in a nice speed boat already looking for Russia "Uh oh!" thought Steve, there was no wind. Steve was praying for wind especially because it was the start of the journey, otherwise they would have to stop the trip.

Two hours later, feeling lucky that he had brought his phone as he saw a plane high, but high enough to take a photo of Non-Frightened Nathan & Forgetful Frank in it.

"Ha!" he blared "Hahaha!" 2 down 2 to go. Except the wind had got stronger but the boat people were ignorant and only asked for the tickets in the middle of the journey, so you could be thrown out of the boat left to sink. That was the problem he forgot to buy a ticket and it was the middle of the journey!!

"Ticket," snapped a man.

Steve's face went crimson. As the man watched vigorously, he finally found out Steve had no ticket!!

"THROW HIM OUT!!!" he bawled, but when he tried to throw him out, he heard a deafening "STOP!"

So the 20th time he stopped, even gravity took notice and stopped but after that another man came and asked "Are you the guy that is trying to go to India without flying and then win £20.000?"

"Yes," he replied back.

He then said, "You look like the rich coder kid."

The man who screamed 'THROW HIM OUT!!!' put him back where he was.

Chapter 4

Two days later, they had reached Russia it was time to reach Mongolia. This would be a hard journey as Russia is the biggest country in the world, he booked a ticket for a taxi, but when he started paying by phone, it said you needed more money to pay for a taxi fare. "Oh Yes!" he then thought, "My phone ran out of battery"

Two hours later, Steve found himself in a bus heading towards Mongolia (he thought anyway). Once the journey had ended they let him exit without a ticket and instead gave him money.

"Thanks," he said.

"You're welcome," they all replied. He knew exactly why this happened. Steve then started sprinting towards some grass ahead of him, but when he got through the grass, he could see impertinent Isaac in front of him, so he started sprinting even faster, Isaac felt a sweaty punch.

Although he fell to the ground by the punch, He did not give up. Instead, he rested for 10 seconds, got up and started sprinting like he was flying. In fact, he was flying!! He got down really quickly impertinent Isaac took a photo of him. Wait a second, as he was flying so quickly, he already reached the end of China. "Boo yeah Boo yeah!" he sang.

Chapter 5

In the blink of an eye, he ended up in a taxi that took him to the finals.

"I am sorry," a man said, "But you came third."

Steve smiled instead of crying and then asked, "How do you know they did not fly?"

Forgetful Frank forgot he flew, but Non-Frightened Nathan remembered, and started sweating in no time. Quickly, Steve got out his phone and showed them the pictures he took.

"Thank you" the man said.

A couple of minutes later another man said. "Congratulations, you are first, here is your £20,000."

"Thank you," he stated with a big sigh of relief.

The Boy Who Said Yes

By George Fowler, 6 years old

Chapter 1. Meet Tomis

Tomis was a boy who said yes. He said yes to everything in the world.

One day he said, "Well today is a new day." Tomis decided he did not want to say yes anymore.

Tomis said no to bread and mayonnaise, he said no to milk and even no to sizzling sausages!

Chapter 2. No

Tomis had a brother. His brother often said NO!

Tomis's poor Mum and Dad were horrified by their own sons saying no all the time. Mum and Dad decided to get revenge!

The next day, Tomis and his brother asked if they could watch Ryan's Toy Review, to the boys' surprise Mum and Dad said…….NO!

Chapter 3. Revenge

Mum and Dad said no to Tomis watching the Grinch Movie.

No to Harry Potter.

No to the Despicable Me Movie.

No to Football.

No to a sloth and a scooter.

No to playing PlayStation.

No to Pokémon Cards.

No to a chocolate bar.

No to tying their laces….

Chapter 4. Yes

Finally, Tomis and his brother realised that if they kept saying no, then Mum and Dad would keep saying no to them too. They wanted their nice things.

So, the boys decided to say YES and so did Mum and Dad.

The End

The Mansion

By Anneliese Gambrill, 10 years old

It was late in the afternoon, when Isabella and Billy were coming home from a long day at school. They lived in the same house, as they were brother and sister, actually, they weren't just brother and sister, they were twins!

They passed a creepy-looking mansion, in a dark, eerie place by the path they were walking along.

"Should we go in?" Isabella asked.

"No!" exclaimed Billy. "Mum said not to go in there!"

After begging for what seemed like forever, Billy finally agreed, but said that if they got caught, it wouldn't be his fault.

As they came closer, the mansion loomed over them. Leafless, brown vines were creeping up the walls, like hands reaching for the sky. The misty windows were smashed, and some were bricked up and the balconies looked lonely and sad. The scent of freshly cut grass caught their noses, and they saw that the grass in the front garden of the mansion was cut...

They looked around to see if there was anybody watching them, but no one could be seen. They carefully crept up the pathway to this ghastly place looking all around as they went.

They cautiously climbed up the moss-covered steps, to find that the door to the huge house, was overgrown with vines and all sorts of plants. They both forced through them, to find themselves in a vast (what must have been) hallway. Cobwebs had been spun in unlikely places, and sitting on the mantel piece, was a picture of an old man, who seemed to be staring straight at them. They stood still.

The man had grey hair (as you'd normally expect on an old person). Although, this one did not have a kind smile on his face, he had an angry frown. It was his stare that was the scariest thing about him. He had piercing bloodshot eyes from which you could not hide.

Suddenly, the vines quickly covered the doorway behind them like a dense thicket, there was no way out...or was there?

"Help!" cried Isabella.

"I want my mummy!" exclaimed Billy shakily.

"We need to find a way out!" said Isabella. They speedily searched for an escape route.

Finally, Isabella spotted a broken window, "Look, that's big enough for us to fit through," she said.

"Great, a way out of this place," responded Billy.

They ran over to it, just as the vines started crawling after them and they climbed out, before the vines completely covered the opening. As soon as they were out, they sprinted as fast they could, all the way home, breathing heavily.

When they reached their house, their mum was waiting at the door for them. She was furious. "Where have you been all this time? I've been so worried!" she said.

"We went a different way," said Isabella.

"And got lost!" said Billy, quickly.

"It's ok, at least you're home now, let's go and have ourselves an early dinner," said Mum giving them a suspicious look.

"I told you it wouldn't be my fault," huffed Billy.

"Ok, ok, I'm sorry," said Isabella, reluctantly.

"It's fine, now let's go and eat, I'm famished," said Billy.

Later that evening, they were speaking about their experience at the mansion. They said to each other that they would never go back there again, and hopefully, never have to see it again.

"Even though we've decided not to go back to that horrible place, I do wonder what happened to that painting and if *it* made the plants move," said Isabella.

"Yeah, me too," Billy said, "Me too."

The Cursed Secret

By Eloisa Beasant, 10 years old

As I stared longingly, at the world outside my window, glistening snowflakes fell transforming the countryside and coating it in a blanket of white.
I jumped, as I heard a howl from outside. I dashed downstairs, slinging my coat over my pyjamas and shoving my feet into my boots. I cautiously peeped round the door wondering what could be out there, only to see my brother stomping through the snow towards the hedge.

I ran after him stumbling in the snow, catching up with him as he crouched down. As I leaned over my brother's shoulder, I saw right there in front of us - a dragon! I stared for what felt like an eternity but must've been only a minute before glancing at Rowan, he was grinning at me.

I saw the tip of the dragon's tail looked bitten and the dragon howled again.

Rowan whispered 'We need to help - but how?"

"Go and get some towels" I replied, taking charge.

Now alone with the Dragon I moved a bit closer mummering calming words and to my surprise it's face softened and it started speaking to me.

"I am Tropicana. I need your help. Please can you help me bandage my tail. But first, while your brother is gone, let me explain the real reason why I'm here. You can understand me because you're special, you have powers that only you can control, but I am here to help guide you through how to use them properly."

"So, I have powers that make me able to understand animals?" I was astounded.

Tropicana continued "Yes, but you can't tell anyone, otherwise I will become cursed and maybe even the person you tell as well, we both might become evil! But beware there are bad things out there who want your magic and will do anything to get it."

I was stunned, but there was no more time for questions because I could hear Rowan coming up the garden path towards us.

"How is it? I've got the towels!" Rowan peered excitedly at Tropicana.

A week later Tropicana was almost fully healed. I wandered towards the garden shed with her breakfast when I saw the grass had been trampled down. Had my parents found her, or had she left us without a goodbye. I wished that everything was ok as I lifted the latch and pulled open the door.

Tropicana howled with fury and lunged at me, I flipped into the air last minute so she crashed head first into the wall behind me. There was another howl as she flew out straight into my brother as he ran out of the house towards the noise. She screeched in delight as she scraped it at his scalp, his blood curdling scream piercing the air as he ran blindly through the garden and into the road clutching his head. He didn't notice the lorry rumbling up behind him. I dived at him, pushing him out of the way as we tumbled head over heels down the bank on the other side of the road.

I lay there scanning my body and nursing the oozing wound on my arm only to look up and see Tropicana. She was gazing gleefully down and circling the field waiting to pounce. This was what she wanted. She wanted me afraid and confused. She thought she had her moment. She thought she had victory. She saw all these things but she should have looked in my heart. Because somewhere in there I knew what I had to do. Could I do it in time? That was a whole other matter.

I started to mind read her thoughts. I was scared by what I heard: 'Kill the human. Get the magic.' So, I began pushing some of my thoughts into her head: 'The human is good. The magic is hers. Tell the human why you are trying to kill her. The human is good.' But I was horrified by her response: 'The human is trying to take me over.' I tried again. She reeled in the sky and dived; I wasn't sure if it had worked and which side she had taken until…

I woke in bed with Tropicana watching from the window, she whispered goodbye and flew away. I was just wondering if I'd ever see her again and what had happened, when mum came in with a squirming bundle in her arms. She plopped down on the end of my bed and handed her bundle to me, a little head poked out and a little puppy climbed onto my lap.

"Is she for me?" I asked.

"Of course, what will you name her?" Mum questioned.

"Tropicana," I replied and the puppy gave a yap and licked my face, making us both laugh.

A Lucky Escape

By Sia Rao, 7 years old

The sky was vibrant, it exploded in a blaze of pink and gold. The ocean was reflecting in the twilight hour. The waves were calm as the tide came in. Deep in the coral reef, lay a charming mermaid. She had striking, long hair. Her scaly tail was vividly green and purple, it gently swayed in the current of the ocean. Further along the infinite sea bed, was a hungry shark searching for some supper.

Above, on the surface, the waves were soaring high in the air; the crest was a huge arch. The mermaid noticed a peculiar shape cutting through the waves. She felt uneasy. Looking closer, she realised it was a pointy fin of a shark. Fear turned her to stone.

As the massive waves crashed in, the fin got closer... and closer... and closer. Terror surged through her as she came face to face with the fierce shark. She gulped. Filled with fear, she froze to the spot. The mermaid had little time to react before the shark struck. She launched herself into the intense waves and fought her way through. She didn't dare stop because the shark was rapidly chasing her.

As the wave met the ocean, the petrified mermaid found herself behind some large rocks. Frantically, she burrowed herself deeper into the rocks. And waited. And watched. Through the rocks, she saw the ravenous carnivore just on the other side. She felt sick with fear; her stomach was tumbling as if a volcano was erupting inside it. She couldn't move, it seemed like forever. But all of a sudden, as if by magic, the sea monster turned its back. The relieved mermaid could hardly believe her luck. Pounding eased in her chest.

Inch by inch, she moved her way out of the rocks, stopping every few seconds to ensure there was no return of the shark. Just then she noticed a gigantic killer whale racing past the rocks in the direction of the shark. She knew she'd had a lucky escape.

Legend of Fangs

By Sharon Cheruvathur, Year 4

Many years ago, in a small village in Siberia, a school piled into a coach and zoomed away on the rocky road for an end of the school year trip. All the kids were looking forward to this trip and especially a girl named Fiona.

Fiona had packed essentials for the trip and had already boarded the bus along with her luggage. Fiona suddenly realised that she had left her favourite doll inside the school. She ran to pick it up but by the time she returned, the coach had already left. This was a trip she didn't want to miss. She saw the bus and thought she could catch it by running behind it. After running for a distance, she decided to walk. She was not sure where she was going and was getting very tired. So, she stopped by the dense woods.

Just at that moment, vicious growls surrounded her. Her eyes widened. Fiona turned her head around to see what was going on. Suddenly she was surrounded by a pack of aggressive wolves.

Fiona trembled and was motionless. She could not scream nor run. She clenched her hands and bit her lips. A beasty wolf came drooling. It grabbed her by the neck and then sped off deep into the woods. Fiona thought that she was going to be dinner. Unexpectedly, it let her go. There was something about her they sensed. Was it her pure heart? Fiona was still trembling with fear. She fell on the ground unconscious.

Fiona woke up and found herself alone. She gazed up at the sky but all she could see were towering trees that embedded the sun. Fiona didn't know where to go. Hearing eerie noises around her, she started to cry. The wolves hearing her wail came for her.

Fiona felt her stomach knot and every nerve in her body was shivering with fear seeing the wolves again. She didn't know what they wanted. The wolves purred around her and comforted her. She was anxious and had mixed feeling on what will happen next. It was time now for the wolves to return back but they didn't want to leave her behind. They nudged her to join them.

Fiona realised that she was all alone and being with the pack would save her. She went with the wolves and joined the pack. The wolves taught her the wolf way and as the legend goes her name was changed from Fiona to… Fangs!

Race You to the Alps

By Krish Pathak, Year 4

Gleaming, the saffron sun beat down on the chequered cobbled streets of London. All the streets where closed off, all the shops were shut and on Westminster Bridge there was an extraordinary sight to see.

As a landmass of competitors lined up waiting for the chime of Big Ben at midday. Amongst the crowd stood a handsome athletic young man, with gorgeous turquoise eyes and wavy ginger hair, dressed as Spider Man, with a webbed back pack, named Tom Davids.

Suddenly tears appeared out of his eyes on to his tanned hands, remembering the fragile porcelain face of his father in the hospital. This made him determined to focus on the big win – twenty thousand smackeroos.

Bong Bong!!! Big Ben rang its chimes, sprinting as fast as he could Tom (Spidey) ran to Waterloo Station, panting like a dog he finally made it to the ticket office, once he'd got his ticket, he strolled to the station platform, his onward journey to Kings Cross for the Eurostar. Smiling to himself, a sweet taste of success was a good start.

Approaching the Eurostar, this amazing aerodynamic awesome train, butterflies fluttered in his stomach, as this was his first adventure on one of these. A short time into the journey the train screeched to a halt! Spidey went flying across the carriage.

"What's going on?!" he yelled.

Then came a calm voice over the tannoy, "Ladies and gentlemen, apologies for the instant stop, there's been a storm and a tree has fallen onto the railway. As we're at Dover station platform, you have a choice to remain on the train or find an alternative route for your forward journey."

Thinking on his toes, not knowing how long it would take for the train tracks to be cleared of the debris, Spidey decided to head on. Finding his way to Dover port, as a ferry could take him across the English Channel.

Luckily as he was a walk on passenger, there was availability. Feeling defeated he slumped his shoulders, looking around at the other opponents ready to go to Calais. In a split second, reminding himself this was only a small detour to his win, he held his head up nice and tall, walked like a cat onto the gang plank into the ferry, where he found a cosy corner, dumped his baggage and himself for the journey ahead.

Soon to approach Calais the weather was still rough, the motion of the waves churned his stomach, he went out onto the deck for some fresh air, lo and behold he couldn't handle it and threw up everywhere!

"Wooooooooaaaah!!!" cried Spidey, as a gush of wind and the rocking boat, nearly blew him over board. He was so relieved to have arrived at Calais port. Upon investigation of the forward journey, he discovered the next train would be the following day, enabling him to chill.

After recovering from the motion blues, Spidey felt peckish and tried the local delicacy, frogs legs, which came out on a fancy bed of lettuce, with a crunchy sea salt coating and slick, slimy snail caviar, hmm, yum.

Boarding a train for Mont Blanc via Lille, would enable Spidey to rest more. With the locomotive manoeuvre, it slowly drowsed his whole body to a slouching position, into a slumbering snooze, 'Zzzzzzzzzzz.'

The opponent a few seats away, watched him closely fall into a dreamy sleep, waiting to steal his train ticket and wallet, which would cause him more stress and delays, "Hee Hee Hee!" said the man.

Feeling fit as a fiddle, and well rested, Spidey was hopeful for the remainder of his race. Progressing towards the exit doors, Spidey realised he didn't have a ticket. "Where the hell is my ticket?" he searched his pockets frantically, finding only a few loose pound notes.

The ticket inspector called the police, Spidey's palms were beginning to sweat and his voice stuttered as he was afraid of what they'd do to him, he had never been in a situation like this before. He didn't have enough money to pay for another ticket.

A tall, stocky, bearded man in a policeman's uniform approached him.

Spidey pleaded, "Please let me go I really need to win this race, I desperately need the money for my father's treatment." Spidey explained he had been pick pocketed. The only way to prove his innocence was If there had been an eye witness, but what was the chance of this?!

As time passed by, Spidey felt downhearted and incapable of winning the race, or funding his father's medical treatment. All his dreams were shattered and came crashing down, like a lightning bolt of thunder. Eventually he was released, he decided not to finish the race as he had no desire to continue. He headed home once his friend had loaned him some money. The excitement of sharing good news with his father was now a tedious task.

Several months later, at the crack of dawn the doorbell rang, DING-DONG!

Half-asleep Spidey mumbled, and fumbled, slipped and tripped down the stairs. "Who on earth could it be this early?" To his surprise it an opponent of the race, accompanied by a police officer.

"Good Morning Sir," said the police officer. "Sorry to disturb you, but we have an update on your alleged swiper in The Alps. After further investigation of the train CCTV, we discovered that Mr Thomas Buckingham, the winner, was the person who robbed you, preventing your completion of the race. He has been charged for this offence, with a gargantuan penalty of twenty thousand pounds. You are now the true winner."

Spidey was gobsmacked and astonished in every possible way. "You what?" replied Spidey. "Pinch me, pinch me, is this real, is this real?" shrieked Spidey.

Hours later Spidey shared this amazing news with his father. Who replied "You were always a winner in my eyes."

Alex's Adventure

By Mohammed Falahul Islam, 9 years old

Next to the famous clock Big Ben, a race was about to begin. An 18-year-old competitor named Alex was racing to Switzerland. Whoever arrived in Switzerland first would win £20,000.

Just before the race a crimson-faced man came up to him and said: "I am going to win you, sucker."

"3,2,1, GO!" the referee shouted. BOOM! The bullet shot out of the gun. The race had begun.

The boy took his bike and rode it to London Victoria station. The boy asked the ticket man "Can I please have a ticket to East Croydon?"

The ticket man replied, "Sorry youngster, London Victoria station is closed for the day."

"OHH," sighed Alex. "You could take the London Victoria underground station," said the ticket man.

"Okay, thanks" replied Alex.

Alex grabbed his bike and started peddling as fast as he could. Now he was panting like a hungry wolf. As soon as he arrived at the underground he ran down, took his oyster card, went to the District line and took the train to Westminster station.

When Alex got on the train he realised he wasn't the only one on the train. The crimson-faced man was sitting right next to him. Alex pretended not to see him, but the red-faced man knew he had seen him.

The man said, "You think you are going to win but I am because I am taking the plane to Switzerland."

Alex couldn't believe what he had heard as it was against the rules of the race to take a plane. Alex replied, "Can you please say that again?" Alex quietly took his phone out of his pocket and started to record the conversation.

The man repeated, "I am taking the plane to Switzerland."

Just then there was an announcement that the train had arrived at Westminster Underground Station. Alex immediately got off the train. He was thinking about why the man would cheat.

There was no time to think and no time to waste. Alex had to go to the Jubilee line which was one minute away from the District line. He was thinking about the man as he arrived at the platform, he realised he had just missed the train. Luckily, there was another train in 5 minutes but if he missed this train, he would have to wait for 58 minutes for the next train.

5 minutes later, the train showed up and everyone got on-board. Alex read the map and it said that there were two more stops to London Bridge.

Alex arrived at the underground station and he had to go to London Bridge station. It was a one-minute walk from where has was. Alex arrived at the station and jumped on the train, there were only 3 stops to his destination. He had arrived at East Croydon station but not Switzerland.

Alex had arrived just in time, the Eurostar was at East Croydon station. He swiftly ran to the platform before he missed the train. "PHEW," Alex sighed. It was time to get traveling.

The journey was about 3-4 hours. It was lunch-time on the Eurostar and Alex had a chicken burger along with a can of Coca-Cola. After having his scrumptious meal he had a nap. When Alex woke up from his nap there was an announcement that they were in SWITZERLAND and the train would arrive at the station in 2 minutes. Alex took all of his belongings and waited for the train to stop. The train had come to a halt. The doors opened and everybody embarked off the train.

When Alex got off the train, he could see mountains covered in snow and people skiing. Now Alex had to get to the finish line and he had to take a taxi. He had immediately spotted a taxi. He shouted "TAXI, TAXI."

The taxi came round to him and Alex asked him if he could take him to Tylecroft Road. Alex hopped in the taxi.

Finally, after a long journey, Alex had reached the finish line.

The taxi driver asked, "Can I have 10 swiss francs please?"

Alex gave him the money and started to run to the finish line. He came second place.

Alex cried, "Ref, the man who came first place cheated and I've got the proof!" Alex took his phone and played the recording of the brief conversation he had with the man on the train.

The man snatched the prize from the referee's hand and ran away. The referee called for security. The crimson face man was stopped by the security at the gates and surrounded by the guards. He was then arrested and instantly sent to jail.

The Ref said, "Congrats, you have won the race!"

Alex replied, "Thank you." He had just won twenty thousand pounds.

Demon's Playhouse

By Max Yeoman, 8 years old

Once upon a time, a boy named Jack had a friend called Albert. Albert came over to play at Jack's house for the first time as Jack and his family had just moved in.

boys went upstairs and started playing with Jack's action men. One of the action men fell out of Jack's hand and as he got up, he touched a bookshelf. Suddenly, it released a secret compartment. The boys were in shock – you should have seen the look on their faces! They were so surprised that the bookshelf opened.

In the secret compartment was an old computer! The boys went up to the computer and on the screen was an angry face. It was an animated pixilated face.

"Play me!" shouted the computer. Next the screen changed to a game called Demon's Playhouse.

"Wow!" said Jack. "Let's play it!"

"Yes!" replied Albert.

Jack started playing the game. Zombies attacked a village. Jack and Albert had to save the village people from the zombies by killing the zombies. A zombie reached out from the screen!

"OH MY GOSH!" screamed Albert.

Jack said, "I'll go tell my Mum!"

Jack and Albert went downstairs to tell Jack's mum and dad.

"There's a zombie in my room!"

"No there isn't" mocked Dad.

"There is…please believe me!"

"No, go back in your room" said Dad.

Jack replied, "What shall we do now?".

"Get your super zapper squirter!" said Albert.

The door creaked open and they stepped quietly into Jack's room.

"Let's shoot them!"

Shhhhhhhhhhh – went the zapper as the water squirted the zombies.

The zombies melted down on Jack's floor, with a fizz and sizzle, a whizz and bubble!

Jack and Albert did a high five!

Happily, they went to the computer and the computer hauntedly said, "You defeated that…see if you can defeat this!"

A blue and white yeti put its head out of the computer and started coming out creepily.

Jack and Albert looked at each other in surprise .

"What do we do now?" said Albert.

"What will defeat him?"

They go back to Mum and Dad.

"There's a big, giant, ugly yeti in my room!" screamed Jack.

Mum said, "No there isn't, go back to your room and play." She was trying to unpack.

They went back upstairs to Jack's room.

"What shall we use now?" questioned Jack.

"I know!" said Albert excitedly.

"Get your pretend sword and start whacking it!"

"Yes, great idea!" said Jack.

Albert screamed, "And you should get your pet tarantula."

"Let's go and defeat that ugly yeti!"

They put the pet tarantula on the floor and it started crawling up the yeti's body and towards its head. It started biting the yeti. Jack whacked the yeti whilst the tarantula bit the yeti's head.

"That will defeat him!" AND IT DID!

They went back to the computer and the angry face appeared again. It spoke "You've defeated me, now you get a reward."

An arm reached out of the computer screen and gave them gold medals.

"Oh my!" said Jack.

"My mum is going to be so proud of this!" said Albert triumphantly.

"Let's stop all this madness." beamed Jack.

They go to Mum and Dad to show them the medals, "Now do you believe us?"

Terror in the Mud

By Dylan Yeoman, 10 years old

It was just a normal day. I was walking to school in my red and blue t-shirt calling out to my friend Sonny. He had overslept again! Knocking on his window, I tried everything to wake him up and to get to school on time. Finally, he awoke and slid out of bed… in his pants, **EEEWWW!**

He slid out of bed and clambered into his clothes as if it was the hardest thing he had ever done, it wasn't! Sonny ran to the door and suddenly came to a halt "Bun-bun!" he shouted nearly forgetting his baby toy that he brought EVERY day, I mean EVERY day. Slowly but surely, he opened the door; stepped out holding his bag in one hand and his teddy in the other.

"Hi Will!" he said to me whilst high fiving me in the air.

"Hi Sonny" I replied flicking his appearance to now and forgetting the whole pants thing. We walked to our normal route to school… the path was closed. AWWW, FADOODLE CAKES!

"OMG Will, you just swore!" he said. Sonny was dumb D.U.M.B, dumb! Like if there was a record for the dumbest person on earth, he would break and set it since the day he was born till he died. He even thought that fadoodle cakes was a swear word, how ridiculous! Obviously, I wouldn't say that to his face, his chubby muscles would launch you from my house (in England) to Australia. I'm only his friend because he scares other bullies away.

As our normal route to school was closed, we tried to get there another way. We went around the corner and in front of us was a gate. It was familiar as we had once tried this route before…but we never went in there because SOMEONE was always scared to go in. We had no choice today. Sonny was shivering like he was in Antarctica and whispering to his stuffed toy, that it was going to be ok.

We pushed on the gates and they CREEEEEEEAAAAAAKKKKED open. The gates were twisted around each other coiling like snakes about to attack. He gulped, closing his eyes in fear.

A man ran out of a house and bellowed at us to stay away and shook his fist in anger. He chased me and Sonny into an overgrown forest. We appeared to be safe, thank goodness.

Suddenly I thought, how were we going to get out?

We ran, speeding through the forest, Sonny and I headed for the light. It started to rain hard and after what seemed like forever, we were finally at the light. Panting from running so fast, we decided to take a rest in the cave. All of a sudden all went dark, I heard Sonny screaming and I knew something fishy was going on. The walls had closed in!

I banged on the walls surrounding us and they were wet and sticky. Punching the side of the cave I hoped I could find a way out. I felt a tip of something sharp stuck in the walls. It was a sword. We rammed our way in with the sword and to my surprise an opening appeared.

We ran out and found a BIG mushroom to sit on- Sonny saw some berries and chucked them down his throat.

"No!" I cried, trying to stop him from eating the berries. "They might be poiso…." but before I could finish the plants contents were in his mouth.

"What?!" Sonny replied with a red smile from the berries.

"Nothing!" I said, huffing in anger.

"Will I die?" Sonny asked frantically.

I muttered under my breath, "Hopefully…"

"What was that Will?" Sonny said.

I pretended to not hear him.

The ground started to shake from a scale of 1 to 100 and the mushroom pushed us off it.

"AAAAAHHHHHHH!" Sonny screamed. "What is happening Will?"

"I don't know but its freaking me out!" I trembled.

Suddenly an arm came out and tapped us on the shoulder. It wasn't an arm, it was the branch of the berry tree, which was now triple its size.

Then all the plants started to mutate and grow gigantic in size.

"AAAAAHHHHHHH!" Sonny and I screeched at exactly the same time.

Sprinting through the forest, we tried to avoid the tentacles of the plants but it was too late! The cave that we went in, which was actually a huge Venus Flytrap, CHOMPED Sonny whole!

"Sonny!" I bellowed. Even though I was his friend, only because he scared other bullies away, I still cared about him very deeply.

Remembering the sword, I grabbed it and charged at the beast!

The sword was so sharp it cut the Venus Flytrap's throat clean open. It gagged and Sonny spewed out of its mouth, covered in purple goo!

He started running around "BLUUUUUURRRRRRRRR!!!!" he waved his arms madly. "I'm covered in purple slime!" he was grossed out.

I ordered him to stop and follow me. WE HAD TO GET OUT OF THERE!

We started running and behind us the tentacles of the other plants were waving around, trying to get us. The Venus flytrap was on the floor, waiting for death to come its way.

Right before me, Sonny was starting to mutate into a hideous plant monster. The red berries he'd previously eaten were turning him into a bush!

I still had the sword in my hand. By accident I caught Sonny's arm, that started bleeding purple and red juice – the purple goo of the Venus Flytrap and the red berries were reacting together….my friend was transforming before my eyes!

I grabbed Sonny, who minute by minute was growing sharp thorns.

Running out of the forest, Sonny caught me with his thorns "OUCH!!!! That hurt."

I looked down and staring back at me was purple goo – I didn't know if this was end….

Stranded on an Island

By Ankit Kathare, 10 years old

I dragged myself up onto the beach exhausted. The ocean heaved as the tempest raged at the darkness. After chocking and belching, I finally coughed up the salt water from my lungs. For an instant, I lay still like a wall, grateful and weary headed and glared out across the lagoon.

The vessel broke up on the reef. The waves slid, like the swish of a curtain onto the powdery white sand. The raging clouds gave out rain at their best. The waves rose higher and higher, thundered nearer and nearer, then broke into a roar of boiling foam and raced to the shore like galloping foam horses.

Far out at sea, like two giants locked in combat, the waves crashed against each other, soaring high in the air, bending first one way than the other. After the furious storm had ceased, I peered into the shadows and could just make out the dim contour of the lofty palm trees.

Sinking into it, the sand was as soft as wool. I was extremely lucky to be washed up next to the cliffs, I could have protection from strong storms. Trampling to the entrance of the forest, I was certain to cherish my experience.

Hearing the deafening sound of birds chirping hurt my ears. Reaching to the sky, the trees were verdant skyscrapers. I saw a particular tree with fruits as arsenic as grass chained on the topmost part of the tree. I could see that one ripe fruit had fallen at the speed of a cheetah. I pierced it open and it was all orange in it with several tiny black seeds in the centre. It tasted similar to a mango!

Night was approaching and I knew that I needed to attach to the cliffs. After the delicious feast of papaya, I found a bunch of bamboos growing nearby. I had a brilliant idea of cutting a bamboo then tying strings to both ends to make a bow. After a while of observing, I heard a howling sound galloping towards me, I knew from the middle of my heart what it was, Jackals!

There was a whole pack of them racing towards me. My heart was pounding like the repetitive bang of a drum. Their breath smelt of outdated ketchup! Their jagged teeth were like the tip of a knife. The leader and followers were after me because I was on their Island. I grabbed hold of my bow and arrow aimed carefully and hoped for the best.

The leader had found peace and the rest of the pack was frightened to death and ran away at the speed of light. I fainted and in morning I was feeling very scared and couldn't wait to get off the island but, how and when would I?

The Great Cure

By Rohan Sai Kurumaddala, 12 years old

As men were charging around towards their control stations, something peculiar was taking place. No man knew what was happening, they were simply clueless! It was a white room with a ginormous screen and computers stationed with men in Khaki uniforms. This was the International Security Base.

"Sir, Something has entered the atmosphere!" screamed a man.

A big burly giant of a man, the General, came up to the big screen and questioned, "What in the world is that?"

"Sir might I ask, should we send special aircraft?"

A simple nod was all that was needed to send some of the most dangerous weapons against their possible threat. As they watched the objects hurtle downwards, their aircraft caught up with it. They couldn't help but fire missiles at it, so much that the air was chargrilled. But, from the explosion it seemed as if the object didn't even have a dent in it. As it crashed down they could do nothing but watch.

"Evacuate the targeted city now!" cried the General.

"Sir we can't!"

As realization dawned on the General's astonished face, he was almost scared to talk. He quickly left the base.

All of this was happening, but on the other side of the world life was peaceful until….

A tall lanky man was walking down a street in London, He was very pale with jet black hair. He walked up to a massive building and the name on the board couldn't go unnoticed. GROCERY KINGS.

As he entered inside a frail old lady said, "Well welcome to grocery kings."

"Come on old lady, just stop!" begged the man.

The old lady chuckled and a door opened behind her. She nodded towards it.

As he entered, he saw a massive sign exclaiming MI6. He went through several security checks and finally landed in front of a massive office. He walked into a glass room only to be greeted by two men who were identically dressed and looked bizarrely identical.

"Jim, here's your next assignment." explained the man on the right. He dashed a file on the table that was painted 'top secret' in red letters. Jim picked it up and skimmed through it.

"UFO's! Really?" he exclaimed.

The men opposite him remained poker faced.

He grabbed the file and shot out of the office, after taking a bagel.

As he reached home, he became wary of people following him. He opened the door to his flat to be confronted by a monk. He looked like a relic, he could at least be 90 years old. The old man gave him a grin and he politely asked Jim to sit down.

He pointed to the man's couch. Jim sat. Jim was nothing but astonished, "How did you get past the security?"

The old man chuckled and explained, "Well let's just say it is the monks way of life!"

The old man swiftly explained to him what happened in the Himalayan region where the UFO landed. Supposedly it landed in the territory which is well known for its terrorists. The old man had a vision that told him that there was part of a cure to coronavirus in that. They were scattered around the world and one of the parts of the cure was there.

Jim listened to all this with patience, but in the end he said, "Listen sir if you need to go to a hospital I can take you".

The old man resisted and told him, "Take a look in your file."

As Jim looked into his file, it said the UFO landed in the Himalayas near terrorist banks. No-one in that town knew about it yet.

Jim ran to his computer forgetting about the old man. Jim shouted across the room calling him. When there was no noise Jim ran back, only to find that the old man disappeared. Jim ran out on the road searching for him. A man in jeans walked past him. Jim asked him "Have you seen an old man in his 90s walk this way?"

The person with jeans looked at Jim like he was crazy. Jim ran back to his house, and the man in jeans snickered. His face slowly changed back into the face of the old man Jim had met and his clothes melted into orange monk drapes. He turned into a bird and flew up into the sky.

Jim booked the first flight to India. As he took the flight he noticed an eagle following the plane. The eagle landed on the plane and changed into a crouched figure of a young man. He ran towards Jim's window. Jim freaked out as the man outside was now inside the plane sitting next to Jim.

"Sup?" said the man next to Jim.

Jim was petrified. Just then he realized he was an MI6 agent. Jim put his hand on his gun holster.

But the young man next to Jim threatened, "I wouldn't do that if I were you."

Jim moved his hand from his gun.

The other man got up and said menacingly, "Man you have no idea what forces you are messing with, just don't try getting the cure, or else!"

A flight attendant got up and pointed at the man and told him to sit down. The man flicked his hand almost like flicking a fly, and the flight attendant flew out of the plane screaming. Everyone in the plane started panicking. The flight attendant came flying back into the plane, in a daze.

The creepy man snarled as another man flew into the plane. It was the same man who was wearing the jeans on Jim's street. The man next to Jim flew out of the window. The man in the jeans waved his hand and all the people in the plane went back to normal. Jim stared at that man as he sat next to him. The man slowly changed form back into an old monk. Jim gasped in exclamation, surprised by what he just saw. Then, Jim fainted and was fast asleep.

He woke up as the plane was landing and he quickly searched for the old man. He came out of the plane into the airport still searching. When he couldn't find him, he gave up and headed for his driver. A man was waiting for him with a Bentley. Jim told him to go to an airfield near the borders of India.

The car trip was long and thankfully no one attacked him. He planned on finding the old man and questioning him. When he reached the airfield an old man came up to him. He was dressed shabbily with aviator goggles on his head. The old man gestured to his house and as Jim entered, he quickly closed the door.

The old man slowly started changing form to the monk that saved Jim's life, "We don't have much time."

Jim was gawking. The old man put his hand on Jim's forehead and slowly Jim disappeared.

Jim felt like he was falling, falling through darkness until finally he materialized on a massive mountain covered in snow. Jim immediately began shivering. The old monk gestured towards Jim and pointed towards a small village beckoning him to come. Jim had no choice but to follow him.

As they reached the village Jim noticed no one was coming outside. The old man led him to a house in the corner of the village, where he saw a man. He hastily introduced himself. His name was Tajik and he was a magician and protector of the world. He protects the world from evil magicians. The world believes their home to be terrorist area but it is actually their prison. They were trapped in there, until now. When that meteorite crashed it broke the magic barrier keeping them inside the prison, but now they are free. He told Jim,

"The cure you are looking for is in that meteorite, but they still live in that area as they now turned it into a fortress."

"Why can't you just go?" questioned Jim.

"Young one I cannot go as that is sacred enemy ground, if I go they will know I am a magician, but if you go they will think you are a lost tourist," explained the monk.

Jim had no other option but to agree. They were to set out for their journey tomorrow at first light. Jim was packing all his guns, but the monk took out the guns, turned them into ants and watched with joy as they scuttled off. Jim couldn't believe what the old man did. The old man told him, "If I could turn them into ants the enemy magicians can turn them into much worse things."

Jim nodded in agreement and set off for his voyage. As he climbed up the mountain he was thinking of a way to get through their defences. Thankfully the monk gave him a black stick that glowed. It was made out of magic so no one could hurt him. As he walked up the mountain, he could see a glowing purple wall. There were many people by this wall. They were all armed with swords, bows and shields. As Jim walked up to them, he felt a prick on his arm, a small dart embedded itself into him. Jim slowly collapsed....

Jim woke up in a small chamber. Everything was going exactly as planned. Jim slowly pulled his stick out of his backpack and cut the bonds on him. He slowly crept out of the cell. He snuck up behind a guard and clubbed him over the head, then took his uniform. He then dashed forward and found himself outside. He put on the guard's uniform and strolled outside casually.

He saw the meteorite, it looked beautiful. It was made out of precious stones and metals; gold, diamond and many more. For a second Jim was overwhelmed by the precious meteorite, but he remembered what he was here for. He walked through a tunnel dug through the meteorite. In the centre of the humongous rock was a tiny flower. The beauty was too much for a human to see.

There were only two guards so before they could blink Jim clubbed them both, expertly took the plant and put it in his backpack. As he stepped outside a battalion of men were standing there waiting for Jim.
The man from the flight in jeans came forward and yelled, "Give me the plant and no-one gets hurt."

Jim resisted against them and knocked out one man. The rest charged at him only to be swept back by extreme winds. THERE WAS A CYCLONE! But the winds weren't affecting Jim. When he looked at that cyclone there was a humanoid figure inside it. The MONK!

Jim quickly ran out of the fortress just before it exploded, creating a giant mushroom in the sky. After he got out of the Himalayas, he got on the first flight he could find and headed to London to present the herb.

5 Weeks later:

Jim was lounging on his armchair in his house. The cure had worked and now he was at peace. He received no word from the monk since the explosion.
He went to his living room to find the monk sitting drinking some tea, "Did you miss me?"

THE END

The Light of day

By Khyati Rahul Oza, 11 years old

"Florence dear, hurry up!" called out a very shrill voice.

"Coming! I'm just bringing my suitcase down!" replied Florence. Florence, a young girl born and brought up in Paris, was going to visit her old grandmother, Zaria, in Nigeria, as she did every summer. Zaria, a rather strong 85 year old lived all by herself in Ilab village cradled in the Niger valley nestled between the hills.

As Florence hurled her suitcase down, she heard her mother and father bickering whether to leave the lights on. Sighing with frustration, Florence grumbled "Ma, Pa, Stop! Why don't you just leave the lights on? We have no dearth of electricity. We have to leave now or else we'll be late!"

After 10 minutes of endless disagreements they were finally able to leave. The car journey was long and tedious as Florence stared at the never ending plains of grass. Once they arrived, Florence's mother and father panicked as they realised that they were an hour behind schedule. After racing around for their security check, they boarded the flight.

Upon reaching their destination, they were greeted by kisses and embraces. Florence scanned her grandmother's abode. It was a pretty cottage with a thatched roof. The curved walls were decorated with flamboyant African art. In the middle of the room was a single lamp.

As the days passed, Florence couldn't bear seeing this poor community struggle. The next night a loud BANG! was heard. A few seconds later the only bulb switched off, the hut drowned in darkness.

Zaria ran out of the house and enquired what happened. A man mumbled it was a power cut. Florence was astonished because she had not experienced one before in Paris. Zaria lit a candle.

The next day Zaria wore a white Kofia, the crown worn by the town chief, embellished with thousands of fantastic feathers. They trooped outside and stood as Zaria sat majestically on her seat. In the middle of the heated meeting, a man stood and yelled that this was a useless village that had unreliable electricity. Others chanted with him. Florence eyed Zaria and was surprised to see her eyes swelling with tears given she was such a strong woman. Florence squeezed her arm trying to reassure her, Zaria announced that she will come up with a solution soon.

Just before going to bed, Florence walked to Zaria and kissed her wrinkled palms and whispered softly. "I think I have an idea iya nla" Florence said with a wry smile. "In school I learned about hydroelectricity. It is electricity made by the flow of the water. We are blessed with Niger. If we collect the water and pass it through a motor, we can make our own electricity. We don't need to rely on the government! We can be self-sufficient!"

Florence's grandmother stared at her awestruck, she took the girl in her arms and kissed her forehead.

The next day, Zaria announced this to the village. Everyone hailed the idea excitedly. Abaze, the village's engineer, whooped with joy and started to work immediately.

Days later it was finished! Florence crossed her fingers hoping it would all work out. Apprehensively, Zaria turned the turbines on. It worked! A wave of light flooded the dark village. A wave of relief washed over Florence as swarms of people clustered around her.

It was as good as the light of day, in the darkness of night.

Lost

By Anoushka Richard, 10 years old

"Good evening! Welcome aboard to Lobenian Airlines to this flight to Florida. This is your captain speaking. I hope you have a wonderful time."

I gave a wriggle of enjoyment as I felt vibrations on my seat. I could hear the squirming noises of the engine warming up. Staring out of the window, a lifeless and melancholy sky had transformed to a pale, cerulean colour blue with candyfloss clouds beneath me and the sun proudly smiling at me.

Half an hour later, while I was browsing some movies an ear-splitting sound was heard. "ALERT! The plane is crashing. Please stay calm and don't panic. Under your seats you will see some equipment and a bag to take with you. Keep safe. Bye!"

Running my hands through my hair, I slid down the staircase arriving at a riverside. There were roughly 2000 people and I couldn't find my way through.

Yawn! I was in a forest. I had wondered why and how I had arrived here. Maybe I came here while I was on my walk. Now I was alone. I was stuck. I was isolated. There was a spidery tangle of trees, bushes, thorns and gnarled limbs.

Cloaked in the mist, like ghostly stooped figures, I heard a sound, my heart pounded. My pulse raced, my eyes widened. There was a massive figure behind me. My jaw was trembling. Chattering like castanets and no matter how hard I bit my lip I couldn't stop. I glanced back. I took a deep breath out. It was only a vast, canopy of treetops formed like a large viridian blanket. Dew soaked grass like a field of jewels licked my ankles. Rotting leaves hid the roots that wriggled across the ground.

Soon I become tired. Exhaustion had made me light-headed. I lay on the floor, dragged down by an irresistible urge to sleep. While I was asleep, a poison had taken over my stomach seeping through my veins and spreading bile to the back of my throat. I couldn't stop it. What would I possibly do? I couldn't do anything and I had no one to help me.

It lasted for 2 hours. Still racked with pain, I couldn't get up to find food. What could I possibly do?

I tried to get up; however, I just couldn't. I had caught a vision. I had never had a vision before, it was about my family. Wait. My FAMILY! It was my family confined in this haunted house. I needed to go to a town near here and try to find food because I was starving. So how would I find my way? There should be someone living in this forest.

I began my journey. Without a second thought, I started to walk down the old, endless, grey path, scattered with leaves and long twigs. Every step I took the lead to a deafening CRUNCH...

The further I went into the forest, the more frightened I got. The tall trees, which were masked by shadows, towered over me, almost like they were watching every step I took. All was silent. No birds chirped, there was no howl of the wind. I started to smell a type of flower. The smell was so strong that I started to get a headache.

The darkness of the forest was thickening. With no light in sight, I tried to get out of the endless maze. Following the path, I ran the back of my hand across all the trees. They felt weird, like coral from under the sea, the moss cold and wet, the bark sharp and bumpy.

My mind turned to where the path would take me. I thought of animals roaming free – colourful birds of all colours flying through the air. I thought of my house and all my family waiting for me with lots of treats for my arrival. Then I started to think about something worse. What if the old, endless path never ends and I'm stuck in the forest forever. Night had arrived. I still hadn't arrived.

As dark, ghostly shadows cast over the deserted, dead forest, I crept slowly towards the bright shine from the otherwise dim sky. Midnight had come. No stars could be seen. In the distance, wolves howled loudly at the moon that was flying high in the sky.

Asking myself why I hadn't defied the temptation of going into the forest, I went on with the little hope left in my heart that I would escape this horror. The only noise that could be heard was the occasional twig snapping beneath my shaking feet and the sudden hoot of an owl calling to her young. This was all enough to make my fear rise even more.

I felt scared. Petrified was the main thing. My journey continued, trees wound around, watching me as I walked. By the minute the forest got darker. And I felt lonelier. I was in a nightmare. I couldn't wake up now because all of this had made me stressed.

I dreaded to think about what could be waiting at the end. But then again, I couldn't help it. I was hoping it would be the escape. But my mind seemed to think it would be something terrible. Torture maybe. Anything. But it could be a land of exotic birds and rainbows and flowers. It sounded nice, but all I wanted was to be at home. Cared for. Warm and safe.

The Runaway Rat

By Chahat Gupta, 8 years old

There was once a tiny, little girl, Amie. She lived in a small village that had lots of cliffs and hills. Amie loved science and wanted to build a magical machine which could make her bigger and stronger.

She tried and tried and then eventually made a magical machine, she decided that she was going to test it on a rat first. So off she went on her way to the stinky dumpster because most rats lived there.

While she was wandering around one little tiny rat grabbed her attention while he squeaked in a corner, munching on leftovers. She immediately thought this rat is going to be my guinea pig. Amie picked up the rat and slid it into her pocket while it tried to escape.

When she arrived home, she placed the rat on her bedside table and shot it with her newly built machine. The rat was acting as if it had just been given an electric shock. Its eyes started to glow red, its tail extended and it started to grow larger.

It started striding towards Amie, she backed away and she hit a wall, and screamed "Help, help me!"

Never before, had she seen a rat that was ten times bigger than her. The rat was frightened with her screaming and felt strange in a huge body. While trying to catch Amie, the rat breathed heavily and Amie's heart was pounding as the rat got nearer to her. She managed to escape and hid under her bed and started thinking quickly what should she do next?

Meanwhile, the rat started briskly walking back towards the stinky dumpster. On his way to his place he grabbed cars and traffic lights and crunched them up. He slurped from engine oil cans for refreshment, followed by a plank of wood as his chocolate dessert.

Amie was calling the police so that they could catch the runaway rat. The police took out the biggest net possible and zoomed away. The car engine roared but the rat was too fast. It dived off the cliff and began swimming in the sea below. The police car somersaulted through the air and landed on the rat's head with a thud. The rat choked from this sudden thud. The police managed to capture the rat but it nearly chewed itself out of the net. They took it to a place where it couldn't hurt anyone.

But Amie at the back of her mind wanted to return the rat back to its old size. Then while worrying she fell asleep. She had a dream which showed her exactly what to do. Her dream told her to say, "Cheeky choky boom, squishy squashy doom," while waving her hands in the air like a magician in front of the rat to bring the rat back!

The next day she plucked up her courage to face the big, strong rat and she was prepared to hit it with a bat, in case the rat attacked. She spotted the big rat and used the magic words, "Cheeky choky boom, squishy squashy doom."

Then, the rat went into a puff of smoke and shrank to its old size. Amie was relieved and she kept the rat as her pet and named him Norman.

The Magical Tree

By Haziq Rizwan, 8 years old

As the sun climbed its way to the top. Derek hopped out of bed. "Ah, a lovely sunny morning to start the day as usual," he said.

As Harold walked into Derek's room, he said, "Derek draw out your curtains because I want to tell you something."

"What is it?" asked Derek drawing out his curtains at the same time. Both brothers were kind hearted though they lived in an unpleasant town.

As Harold was about to speak BANG! BANG!

"What's that? It sounded creepy," said Derek in fright.

"Don't be such a baby, I'm sure it was nothing," replied Harold with a laugh. They both went towards the window and looked outside.

"What are you looking at?!" snapped their neighbour her eyes looking fierce.

Harold pulled the window backwards. Their neighbour was very rude, she hated having neighbours. She didn't like other children but she loved hers.

"Anyways, back to what I was saying. We're moving to the country!" said Harold eager to see Derek's re-action.

"YES!" exclaimed Derek jumping up and down waving his arms about. He sang "We're going to move away, from clockwork town and go to, paradise!"

"Let's go and have breakfast first," said Harold.

In an hour's time they arrived at the station. Derek always called the town clockwork because they live next to factories with smoke coming from their chimneys. As they sat on the train, they waved goodbye to their town. How they hated the town!

When they arrived at the station they had to walk 2 miles! "My God this is a long walk. I shall fall down half way!" said Derek in shock.

"Don't worry Derek," replied his mother.

"Father," said Harold, "Isn't there any transport to take us?"

"No son," he said in a rather unlucky voice.

"Let's start then," said Harold, sighing.

Half way, Derek was dragging his feet and so was Harold. When they reached the new house Harold said, "I'm going to rest."

Derek however said, "I don't want to miss Batman vs Joker final combat, so I want to ask you if I can or can't watch TV?"

"You can," replied his mum. Just then a van pulled up, it placed all the furniture in the room in less than two hours.

The next day they got up and, oh there were so many chores to do! There was homework from their tutor and school teacher. Derek was accused of pouring oil on the floor so when the teacher came, he would slip over. Then he was given double homework to do.

Derek kept asking his mum when they could explore the forest. She just said tomorrow or no. "When can we go mum?" asked Derek for the twentieth time.

"Tomorrow," she replied carrying on her dishwashing.

When the moon rose in the sky and the stars filled the dark. Derek woke up and looked outside and spoke to himself. "I wonder if I should wake Harold?"

"Derek, would you like to come with me to the forest?" asked Harold suddenly appearing behind him.

"Harold where did you come from?" asked Derek turning round.

"I woke up to go to the toilet when I heard your voice Derek," said Harold. "Shall we go to explore the forest?"

"Oh yes please!" replied Derek.

"Ok then, get dressed first and don't make a single sound!" replied Harold looking stern.

In about a minute they stood outside their cottage all dressed in their normal clothes. So they ran towards the forest and saw a door so tiny that they had to lay down. Derek touched the door and it shot open. They then stood up and saw a door size of their length and went through it.

They saw a large old tree standing in front of them which had ropes let down and bright lanterns hung on the tree. They climbed the ropes and saw parties going on inside tiny houses.

"What is this?" said Derek. In a minute or less a waterfall came down the tree spreading out like an eagle spreading its wings.

Harold climbed higher. "Derek hurry up before the water throws you down!" shouted Harold.

Derek was unaware of what was happening and was in a different world. Just in time Harold grabbed Derek's arm and WHOOSH went the waterfall splashing onto the floor. Harold pulled him up and shook him hard. "Dude you almost fell!" he said shaking him harder.

Derek blinked. "Sorry Harold," muttered Derek embarrassed.

They then walked across the green floor and came to a set of aeroplanes. Two people came out of them with shopping bags. "Hello Harold and Derek," said the two people together.

"Who are you and how do you know our names?" questioned Harold.

"My name is Triangle Head and this fairy's name is Florence," replied Triangle Head smiling. He was as tall as the children and had a Triangle Head that is why his name was Triangle Head.

"Would you like to come on a ride?" asked Florence. She had short golden hair which fell behind her and had a dark green suit with circles at the top.

"Ok then," said Derek who couldn't wait any longer. They hopped inside an aeroplane which looked like a first class aeroplane. They arrived at an enormous shopping mall which was as large as five mansions on top of each other! The doors were their size but the shopping mall wasn't! To an even bigger surprise it wasn't a shopping mall it was a city!

"My God am I dreaming?" questioned Derek to himself.

"No you aren't," said Triangle Head laughing. Together they ate ice-cream and enjoyed mango juice.

"Derek! Didn't you realise it's five thirty! Mum will check us in fifteen minutes! Quick!" shouted Harold.

They raced out of the door of the mall and leapt into the plane. Triangle Head safely landed outside their house and the children raced inside to their bedrooms.

The Story of The Woods

By Bella Young, Year 5

She walked towards the lonely, mysterious woods, wondering how her grandmother could live in such a place. It was beautiful and all but it didn't seem to her to be a dream home, it had some ups and some downs; for starters it had blinding light streaming from the sky and vines curling around the trees ruining the view. The sky was clear but had fluffy clouds drifting around the area, she paused, then her jaw hit the floor, she stopped in her tracks and stared for a while and imagined what would be ahead of her past the archway she had just spotted.

She got closer and stepped inside then she fell to her knees. She had just seen the most unforgettable sight, her knees trembled then her arms and soon she was shivering, her Grandma's town was destroyed.

Then night fell, the moon stared at her like a snake's eye eager to pounce but wearily she looked away. She had had enough of this for now and decided she would carry on and ignore it. She walked. As she got closer to a cave she thought she would tuck in for the night and got closer, then she heard a loud noise coming from that direction… she peered inside and found out the noise was just a bunch of bats squealing. She shooed them off and dropped to the ground already fast.

In her dreams she was in the place she had collapsed but something was off, she heard howls in the wind and her cosy spot was the only place not surrounded in deadly red light. The howls got louder as if coming from the buildings and shadows curled around her.

She awoke in a pool of sweat, her heart pounding like a drum, she looked around her and realised she hadn't woken up, or so she thought, she ran and ran – spotting her grandmother's house she ran inside.

Her Grandma asked her what was wrong, her face turned to shadow and she ran out of the house screaming for her life as all she loved was swept away.

She finally woke screaming or was she still asleep?

Printed in Great Britain
by Amazon